HUMBLE PIE

Gordon Ramsay
HUMBLE PIE

HARPER

Harper
An Imprint of HarperCollins*Publishers*
77–85 Fulham Palace Road,
Hammersmith, London W6 8JB

www.harpercollins.co.uk

First published by HarperCollins*Publishers* 2006
This edition 2007

1

The Author asserts the moral right to
be identified as the author of this work

A CIP catalogue record for this book
is available from the British Library

ISBN-10 0-00-722968-2
ISBN-13 978-0-00-722968-0

Printed and bound in Great Britain by
Clays Ltd, St Ives plc

This book is proudly printed on paper which contains wood
from well managed forests, certified in accordance with
the rules of the Forest Stewardship Council.
For more information about FSC,
please visit www.fsc-uk.org

Mixed Sources
Product group from well-managed
forests and other controlled sources
www.fsc.org Cert no. SW-COC-1806
© 1996 Forest Stewardship Council
FSC

To Mum,
from cottage pie to *Humble Pie*
– you deserve a medal.

CONTENTS

FOREWORD

IN MY HAND, I've got a piece of paper. It's Mum's hand-writing, and it's a list – a very long list – of all the places we lived until I left home. I look at this list now, and there are just so many of them. My eye moves down the page, trying to take in her spidery scribble, and I soon lose track. These places mean very little to me: it's funny how few of them I can remember. In some cases, I guess that's because we were hardly there for more than five minutes. But in others, it's probably more a case of trying to forget about them as soon as possible. When you're unhappy in a place, you want to forget about it as soon as possible. You don't dwell on the details of a house if you associate it with being afraid, or ashamed, or poor – and as a boy, I was often afraid and ashamed, and always poor.

Life was a series of escapades, of moves that always ended badly. The next place was always going to be a better place – a bit of garden, a shiny new front door – the place where everything would finally come right. But it never did, of course. Our family life was built on a series of pipe dreams – the dreams of my father. And he was a man whose dreams always turned to dust.

I don't think people grasp the whole me when they see me on television or in the pages of some glossy magazine. I've got the wonderful family, the big house, the flash car in the drive. I run several of the world's best restaurants. I'm running round, cursing and swearing, telling people what to do, my mouth always getting me into trouble. They probably think: that flash bastard. I know I would. But it's not about being flash. My life, like most people's, is about keeping the wolf from the door. It's about hard work. It's about success. Beyond that, though, something else is at play. Is it fear? Maybe. I'm as driven as any man you'll ever meet. I can't ever sit still. Holidays are impossible. I've got ants in my pants – I always have had. When I think about myself, I still see a little boy who is desperate to escape, and anxious to please. The fact that I've long since escaped, and long since succeeded in pleasing people, has made little or no difference. I just keep going, moving as far away as possible from where I began. Where am I trying to get to? I wonder . . . Work is who I am, who I want to be. I sometimes think that if I were to stop, I'd cease to exist.

This, then, is the story of that journey – so far. The tough childhood. My false start in football. The years I spent working literally twenty hours a day. My battles with my demons. My brother's heroin addiction. The death of my father, and of my best friend. I'm just forty, and it seems, even to me, such an amazingly long journey in such a short time.

Will I ever get there? You tell me.

CHAPTER ONE
DAD

THE FIRST THING I can remember? The Barras – in Glasgow. It's a market – the roughest, most extraordinary place, people bustling, full of second-hand shit. Of course, we were used to second-hand shit. In that sense, I had a Barras kind of a childhood. But things needn't really have been that bad. Mostly, the way our life was depended on whether or not Dad was working – and when I was born, in Thornhill Maternity Hospital in Johnstone, Renfrewshire, he was working. Amazingly enough.

Until I was six months old, we lived in Bridge of Weir, which was a comfortable and rather leafy place in the countryside just outside Glasgow. Dad, who'd swum for Scotland at the age of fifteen – an achievement that went right to his head, if you ask me – was a swimming baths manager there. And after that, we moved to his home town, Port Glasgow – a bit less salubrious, but still okay – where he was to manage another pool. Everything would have been fine had he been able to keep his mouth shut. But he never could. Sure as night followed day, he would soon fall out with someone and get the sack; that was the pattern. And because our home often came with his job, once the job was gone, we were homeless. Time to move. That was the story of our lives. We were hopelessly itinerant.

What kind of people were my parents? Dad was a hard-drinking womaniser, a man to whom it was impossible to say 'no'. He was competitive, as much with his children as with anyone else, and he was gobby, very gobby – he prided himself on telling the truth, even though he was in no position to lecture other people. Mum was, and still is, softer, more innocent, though tough underneath it all. She's had to be, over the years. I was named after my father, another Gordon, but I think I look more like her: the fair hair, the squashy face. I have her strength too: the ability to keep going no matter whatever life throws at you.

Mum can't remember her mother at all: my grandmother died when she was just twenty-six, giving birth to my aunt. As a child, she was moved around a lot, like a misaddressed parcel, until, finally, she wound up in a children's home. I don't think her stepmother wanted her around, and her father, a van driver, had turned to drink. But she liked it, despite the fact that she was separated from her father and her siblings – it was safe, clean and ordered. The trouble was that it also made her vulnerable. Hardly surprising that she married my father – the first man she clapped eyes on –

when her own family life had been so hard. She just wanted someone to love. Dad was a bad lot, but at least he was her bad lot.

By the age of fifteen, it was time for her to make her own way in the world. First of all, she worked as a children's nanny. Then, at sixteen, she began training as a nurse. She moved into a nurses' home – a carbolic soap and waxed floors kind of a place – where the regime was as strict as that of any kitchen. In the outside world, it was the Sixties: espresso bars had reached Glasgow and all the girls were trotting round in short skirts and white lipstick. But not Mum. To go out at all, a 'late pass' was needed, and that only gave you until ten o'clock. One Monday night, she got a pass so that she could go highland dancing with a girlfriend of hers. But when they got to the venue, the place was closed. That was when the adrenalin kicked in. Why shouldn't they take themselves off to the dance hall proper, like any other teenagers? So that was what they did. A man asked Mum to dance, and that was my father, his eye always on the main chance. He played in the band there, and she thought he was a superstar. She was only sixteen, after all. And when it got late, and time was running out and there was a danger of missing the bus, all Mum could think of was the nightmare of having to ask the night sister to take her and her friend back over to their accommodation. Then he and his friend offered to drive them back in his car. Well, she thought that was unbelievably exciting, glamorous even. He was a singer. She'd never met a singer before.

After that, they met up regularly, any time she wasn't on duty. When she turned seventeen, they married – on 31 January, 1964, in Glasgow Registry Office. It was a mean kind of a wedding. No guests, just two witnesses, no white dress for her, and nothing doing afterwards, not even a drink. His parents were very strict. His father, who worked as a butcher for Dewhursts, was a church elder. Kissing, cuddling, any kind of affection was strictly forbidden. My Mum puts a lot of my father's problems in life down to this austere behaviour. She has a vivid memory of a day about two weeks after she was married. Her new parents-in-law had a room they saved for best, all antimacassars and ornaments. Her father-in-law took Dad aside into that room, and her mother-in-law took Mum into another room, and then she asked Mum if she was expecting a baby.

'No, I'm not,' said Mum, a bit put out.

'Then why did you go and get married?' asked her new mother-in-law.

I've often asked Mum this question myself. It's a difficult one. I'm glad I'm here, obviously. But my father was such a bastard, and he treated her so badly, that it's hard, some-times, not to wonder why she stayed with him. Her answer is always the same. 'He wanted to get married, and I thought "Oh, it would be nice to have my own home and my own children".' But she knew he was trouble, right from the start.

Ten months later, my sister Diane came along, and Dad got the job at a children's home in Bridge of Weir. They were given a bungalow on the premises and my poor mother really did think that all her dreams had come true. There was a swimming pool in the grounds, where he was an instructor and manager. According to Mum, it was lovely – idyllic, even. Then it started – the drinking and the temper. She found out that even as they had been getting married, Dad had been on probation for drinking and fighting – though he told her that it wasn't his fault and, like an idiot, she believed him. She was madly in love, you see. The violence against her started soon after that. He would slap her about and, not having had any other experience with men, she assumed that this was what every woman had to put up with. When her father told her that Dad was bad, she refused to believe him. She'd pay a visit home and, when she took off her coat, there were bruises on her arms, and maybe a cut to her eye or her lip.

'Oh, I just banged into a cupboard, Dad,' she'd say. He'd accuse her of telling lies, of covering up. But she was deaf to it all, of course.

Next was the job in Port Glasgow. The prodigal son returns. Dad had all sorts of big ideas about that – his swimming career meant that everyone in the town knew him. They got a nice council house, and I think Mum felt quite settled. But Dad was all over the place – 'fed up' he used to call it, a pathetic euphemism. The womanising got steadily worse – he'd go out at night, and not come back until the morning. Then he'd get changed and go straight off to the pool to work. By now, I was around, and Mum was pregnant with my brother, Ronnie. One morning, Dad came home and announced that his car had been stolen. He made a big show of phoning the police to report it. Of course, it was complete bollocks. What had actually happened was that he'd been with a woman, had a few drinks, and knocked down an old man in what amounted to a hit-and-run. Despite his best efforts, it wasn't long before the police found out and it was all over the papers. There was nothing else for it. Port Glasgow wasn't a very big place, and it was certainly too small for us now. We had to leave, literally overnight. Diane was toddling, I was in a pushchair, and Mum was pregnant. But did he care? No, he didn't. It was straight on the train to Birmingham, and who knows why. It could just as easily have been Newcastle, or Liverpool. He may as well have stuck a pin in a map, at random. We knew no one. We spent the night at New Street Station, waiting for the sun to come up so that Dad could walk the streets, looking for somewhere to live. What a desperate sight we must have made; you can all too easily imagine people walking past, looking down at the pavement in their embarrassment.

We found a room in a shared house. Amazingly, Dad

only got probation and a fine for the hit-and-run, and he soon picked up a job as a welder. The room was horrible, or so Mum tells me, but we just had to make the best of it. We shared a kitchen – in fact, a cooker in the hall – and a bathroom with another family. Meanwhile, Dad joined an Irish band, and all the usual kinds of women were soon hanging onto his every word. If he went out on a Friday night, you were lucky if you saw him again before Sunday. Needless to say, the welding soon went by the way. He wanted to spend more time with the band; he was convinced, despite all evidence to the contrary, that he was going to be a rock-and-roll star. Even at such a young age, these fantasies of his would make me sick. We'd spend time with him going from market to market looking for music equipment. The money he used to spend was extraordinary, and hard to take. There we'd be, looking at these Fender Stratocasters and Marshall amplifiers – the fucking dog's bollocks of the music world – and we'd be dressed in rags. All our clothes were from jumble sales, our elbows and knees patched over and over again. How did he fund his shopping habit? Loan sharks, mostly. His debts still come back to haunt me now – our names are the same, and I'll occasionally get investigated by companies trying to recoup the cash he owes them.

The older I got, the harder this kind of treatment got to bear. I remember when Choppers and Grifters were the big things. Well, of course, we never, ever had a new bike. On birthdays, I used to get a £3.99 Airfix model kit. However much I enjoyed putting those things together, you could tell they'd come from somewhere like the Ragmarket, which was Birmingham's version of the Barras. There'd be half of it missing, or the cardboard box it came in would be so wet and soggy that you wouldn't have wiped your arse with it. Christmas was terrible. When we were older, Mum always used to work in a nursing home, doing as much double-time as she could, sometimes not even coming home on Christmas Day. I used to dread Christmas.

And then the bailiffs would show up. We'd be evicted, Dad's van would be loaded up, and that would be it. Off to the nearest refuge, or round to the social services pleading homelessness. He was always telling them that he was ill, trying to get sickness benefit. In reality, though, he'd be out gigging three or four times a week.

As a teenager, I used to be ashamed of some of the places we lived. We always seemed to end up in the worst of places: the ones that were riddled with damp, with nails exposed everywhere, the ones that had been left like pig-sties by other families. I never used to let on to girlfriends – I'd make them drop me off round the corner. It wasn't so much that I was embarrassed about living on an estate, or in a tenement block. It was more the state of our home itself. Every time he got violent, any ornament, any present we'd bought for Mum, a vase or a picture frame – anything nice – would be smashed or thrown through a window or destroyed, simply because it belonged to her.

I think we built up a lot of insecurity as children. I used to find it so intimidating, walking into yet another new school. Academically, we were never in one place long enough to develop any kind of attention span – and in any case, Dad was hardly the kind of man to insist on you doing your homework. Only poofs did homework. The same way only poofs went into catering. No, he was much more interested in trying to turn us into a country version of the Osmonds. Diane, Ronnie and Yvonne, my younger sister, all sing and play musical instruments. They didn't really have any choice about that, Dad was obsessed. But something in me wasn't having it, and I never went along with his plan. That's not to say I wasn't just as scared of him as they were. My tactic was to keep my head down and my nose clean. I never drank or smoked, and when I was asked to lug his bloody gear about the place, I just got on with the job. It's ironic, really, that people think of me as so forceful and combative, a real aggressive bastard, because that's the precise opposite of how I was as a kid. Until I was big enough to take him on in a fight, I wouldn't have said 'boo' to a goose.

His favourite punishment was the belt. You'd get whacked on the back of your legs with it for something as innocent as going into the fridge and drinking his Coke. I say 'whacked'. The truth is, I would get completely fucked over for that sort of thing. But what would really set him off were lies. I'd lie about things because I was too scared to tell him the truth, 'Yeah, Dad, it was me who went in the fridge and took your Coke' – and then he'd go absolutely fucking ballistic. Of course, what I didn't realise at the time was that it wasn't so much the Coke he was bothered about as the fact that he wouldn't have a mixer for his precious Bacardi. He was the kind of drinker who couldn't open a bottle without finishing it. You'd watch the stuff disappear, and your heart would sink.

Yvonne was born in Birmingham. One night, when Mum was six months pregnant, a neighbour had to call the police as Dad was dishing out some domestic violence on Mum. He was taken away. Mum was taken to hospital and ended up signing consent forms for the three of us to be taken into a children's home for ten days. She visited every day. Then Dad was released and he came back home.

Next stop was Daventry, where we had quite a nice council house. It even had a garden. This time, Dad got a job as a rep, but he was still doing his band work and, thanks to the buying of yet more equipment, the debts were building. One day, he told Mum to pack – only the belong-ings she could fit in his precious van – and we were off again, to Margate where, for a time, we lived in a caravan. He never explained, or tried to justify his behaviour. We did as we were told. That was easily the worst place we ever lived, horrendous. I shudder to think of it. We didn't even have enough money for the gas bottle to keep the place warm. The rain just came pelting down, while inside we shivered, and wondered how long we were going to be there. We were saved by the council, who put us back into a bed-and-breakfast.

Then it was back up to Scotland again, followed by another stint in Birmingham, and then on to Stratford-upon-Avon. Dad had somehow managed to get another job at a swimming pool. But he couldn't settle. Off he'd go: off to France, to America. He never sent money home; it was up to Mum to earn our keep. When he came back from his stint abroad, we moved to Banbury, Oxfordshire, where he was going to run a newsagent's shop. Everything was great for a while. We lived above the shop, and the guy who owned it was lovely. This was Dad's big chance to get it right, if you ask me. But no, he had to screw it all up. One day, while I was getting something out of the fridge, I noticed that the lining of the door was loose. Unnaturally loose. And something was hidden in there – a wad of cash, it must have been at least £300. I remember feeling very sick, I nearly threw up then and there. Dad was on the fiddle. Not long after that, of course, the owner found out, and we were out on our ear again.

So then it was back up to Scotland – Glasgow. Dad had heard that the country and western scene was better up there. But I was a teenager by now, and I decided not to go. The council gave Diane and me a flat and so we stayed put. I was doing a catering course at college, sponsored by the local Round Table who'd even helped me to buy my first set of knives – but, in any case, I don't think Dad wanted either of us around. He just couldn't control Diane the way he'd controlled Mum, and that left him feeling frustrated because in the old days she'd sung with him, been dragged around all the seedy clubs. He had thought she was his, and when it turned out that she wasn't, that she had a mind of her own, he just couldn't take it. Later, when Diane got married, she didn't want him anywhere near her. It was me who gave her away.

As for me, I was public enemy number one. Up in Glasgow, Mum would have to sneak out of the flat if she wanted to ring me. I certainly wasn't allowed to ring her. I had finally crossed a line when I was fifteen. I was going out with a girl called Stephanie, and one night I came back late – too late, in his eyes.

'Get your stuff out of my house, and go and live with her,' he said.

'I'm sixteen next week,' I said. 'I can go where I like.'

I'd already been given some kind of big radio for the upcoming birthday, and he threw it at me, from the top of stairs. 'I can't believe you've done that,' I said. 'You know damn well that Mum bought it for me.' I knew she'd got it on hire purchase, which was costing her £8 a month, and I couldn't bear it. 'I'd rather you did that to me than to something that hasn't even been paid for,' I said.

At that, he came storming down the stairs. At first,

I stood my ground. Then I saw the look in his eyes. That was why I bolted, and I'm not ashamed to admit it. I don't think that I would be here today if I'd stopped and tried to confront him. For the first time, I felt that he really might kill me. I remember him teaching me how to swim by holding my head under the water for minutes on end – I'd end up struggling and gasping for air – so I'd always known he was a sadistic bastard. But I saw something different in his eyes that day – a glint that chilled me. There was nothing there. It was a kind of madness.

Of course, once Diane and I were out of the way, he turned his attention to whoever else was available. Ronnie was his pal, mostly, so now it was Yvonne's turn to take the sort of treatment that I had suffered previously.

By that time, I was already trying to make headway as a cook, on the first rung on the ladder, busting my nuts in a kitchen, and it was unimaginably painful – hearing this stuff from Mum, her voice down the telephone. Yvonne had grown up more quickly than the rest of us – she had a baby in her teens, and she was a real 'ducker and diver', but he just pushed her too far, there was too much pressure, and she was going under.

Meanwhile, Mum was still getting knocked about. She was working in my Uncle Ronnie's shop in Port Glasgow – he was a Newsagent – and she'd come in early in the morning, sometimes not having been to bed at all, with bruised lips and black eyes, and my uncle would say: 'Oh,

Helen, you can't serve the customers looking like that,' and she'd say: 'Well, it was your brother that did this to me.' But, of course, no one intervened. It was a different time then. Domestic violence was still considered a private matter, something for couples to sort out between themselves.

'That's bloody terrible,' he'd say. 'You should hit him back.'

Fat lot of good that advice was. Things got so bad that Mum finally worked up the courage to leave him, and the council gave her, Ronnie and Yvonne a flat. But Dad was soon back, pleading forgiveness, promising that everything would be different. And so it would be, for a few weeks. Then he'd start sliding again, back to his old ways, all this anger always pouring out of him. Oh, he was good at crying crocodile tears, but his heart was an empty space where all the normal feelings a man has for his family should have been.

Next, they embarked on some kind of house swap, and the four of them ended up in Bridgwater in Somerset. Same old story . . . No sooner had they settled in than Dad was off again – this time on a cruise ship. He took Diane with him, to sing, which put Mum's mind at rest a little because even after everything he'd done to her, she was still worrying that he would run off with someone else, and she had this idea that a cruise would be full of beautiful women. Diane was engaged by this time, and her fiancé and Mum saved up to go out and meet the ship in Venice. Mum worked so hard – she had three part-time jobs on the go all at the same time. But when they got there, no sooner had they boarded the ship than Dad had some big, drunken argument with the man who was in charge of the entertainment. This ended with Dad, in a fit of pique, sabotaging all the ship's musical equipment, at which the captain told him he had to leave. They all came back to London by bus – a fine end to Mum's dream trip. Did he feel bad about this? Did he feel guilty? Not at all. He had got his revenge, and that was all that mattered.

It was in Bridgwater that he committed the final transgression, and departed our lives – almost for good, if not quite. It's a time I cannot think about without feeling the blood pulsing in my temples, though I was not even there when it happened. I'm not sure what I'd have done if I had been.

Dad had had a couple of drinks, but he certainly knew what he was doing; this attack was calculated, clever even, not some dumb, drunken rage. He came home from work one night, and he just started. There was no 'trigger'. Mum was in bed, with a mug of hot milk. He poured it all over her, even as she lay there, leaving bad scalding to her chest. Then he dragged her downstairs, and the beating started. By the time the ambulance arrived, she looked like she'd done five rounds with a heavyweight boxer. Her eyes were completely closed, her face swollen and pulped. First, she was taken to a hospital, then to a refuge. Dad, of course, didn't stay to face the music. He disappeared at the first sound of a police siren.

A few days later, I finally tracked him down. He was with a woman called Anne, whom he would later marry.

'Mum's been in hospital for three days,' I said. 'And she's still wearing sunglasses.'

'Well, she asked for it,' he said.

That was when the social services and all the other authorities got fully involved, and a restraining order was taken out on him. He wasn't allowed anywhere near the house.

But when Mum went home, she found everything that she had built up and saved for smashed to smithereens. He hadn't left as much as a light bulb intact.

Worst of all, Dad had left a note on the mantelpiece. It said: 'One night, when you are least expecting it, I'll come back and finish you off'. Even after the restraining order came into effect, there were some evenings when Mum would be sitting in alone and the phone would ring and she'd hear his voice telling her that he was on his way. Many nights, you would have seen a patrol car parked outside the house, just in case. How she slept, I'll never know.

Journalists have often asked me whether I loved Dad, whether I had any love at all in my heart for him. The truth is that any time I tried to get close, I'd just come up against this competitive streak in him. Later, my feelings for him hardened into hatred. Everything he did, I was determined to do the opposite. I never wanted to follow in his footsteps, and that's why I never picked up a fucking guitar, and that's why I never sat at the fucking piano. Were there any good times? Not really. I suppose the only thing that I really admired about him was the fact that he was a fisherman. He was a great fisherman, there's no two ways about it. But even that got tainted by all the other stuff.

Ronnie was good at keeping Dad's secrets, but I made the mistake of telling Mum exactly what he used to get up to. After that, I was never taken fishing again. We used to go to this campsite on the River Tay in Perth – salmon fishing. Ronnie and I would be sitting on the riverbank at nine o'clock at night on our own, fishing, while Dad and his mate Thomas would be out drinking. He'd give us a fiver between us, and tell us to keep ourselves amused. I remember one time when the weather was bad, it was raining heavily, and we'd booked into this little bed-and-breakfast. That night, Ronnie and I ended up sleeping in the bathroom because Dad had brought some woman back. I can't have been older than twelve at the time.

After a while, Dad went off to Spain, and I didn't see him for many years. I was too busy trying to make a success of my life, but even if I hadn't been working every hour God sent, I had no real wish to see him. Dad, though, had a way of turning up when you least expected him, like a bad penny. It was towards the end of 1997. I was busy trying to win my second Michelin star by this point – which should give you some idea of how much time had passed – when I got a call from Ronnie telling me that Dad was in Margate. He'd had an argument with Anne, and Anne's sons, and he'd upped and left.

I called him on the number Ronnie had given me – I don't know why. He sounded very low.

'I'm here to see my doctor,' he said.

'Come on,' I said. 'Why are you really here?'

'No, I'm back just to have a check-up.' There was a pause. Then he said: 'Can I see you?'

'Yeah, yeah, I'll come down.'

It had been a difficult year. My wife, Tana, and I were expecting our first baby. And I was involved in all sorts of legal wrangles over my restaurant, Aubergine. Still, I drove down there. There was something in me that couldn't refuse his request. We were to meet on the pier where we used to go fishing back when we had lived in the town ourselves, so I knew exactly where he'd be. I got out of my car and I saw this old, frail, white-haired man with bruises on his face, and marks on his knuckles. I felt stunned. This was the man I'd been scared of for so long, brought so low, so pathetic and feeble.

We went and had breakfast in a little café. The waiter came over and asked us what we would like and, straight away, Dad started into me, telling me that when I was at home I always used to steal his bread. The words came out of nowhere. Another unwarranted attack.

'What's happened to you?' I said.

'Oh, Anne and I separated, and I had an argument with one of her sons and he tried to have a go at me.'

'Look at the state of you. Where are you living?'

He pointed at the car park, and there, as ever, was his Ford Transit van. We went out and I opened it up and inside there were all his possessions: his music equipment, his clothes, and these silly lamps – paraffin lamps – and an inflatable camp bed in the back with these awful net curtains in the windows.

We finished our breakfast, and we went for a walk on the pier, and it was so sad. So I went to the bank, and I got out £1,000 and I gave it to him for the deposit on a flat. I thought that at least I could do the right thing by him. And that's what he did, he got a little one-bedroomed basement flat. A week later, I went back to see him again. He told me that he was going to be on his own for Christmas. I was in two minds as to what to do. Then I decided: this is not the right time to introduce him to Tana. I felt sorry for him, real pity, but nothing more. And anything I did feel had nothing to do with him being my father; I just felt sorry that a man had to be on his own at that time of year. It seemed so desolate, so bleak.

On Christmas Eve, he telephoned. Anne was coming over to spend the week with him, and they were going to try and resolve their differences. That was the last time I ever spoke to him. Looking back, I wonder if he knew that his time was running out. He'd gone back to Margate because that was where he'd gone on holiday with his parents, as a boy. Perhaps it had happy memories for him. It certainly didn't for me. Driving back to London after that last visit, I cried my eyes out. What a waste of a life.

After hearing that he and Anne had made up, I booked him a table at Aubergine for the 21st of January, 1998. That was going to be a big, big day for me. First of all, that was Michelin Guide day. The new edition. Second, I was going to introduce this guy, my father, to all my staff. I'd spoken of him so little, most of them didn't even know I had a father. The truth is that he embarrassed me. When I was eighteen, a girlfriend gave me a gold chain, a massive gold chain – bling before bling was invented – and Dad was envious of it, so incredibly envious. One day he asked me if he could wear it. So I gave it to him. That was the kind of power he had because at the time I loved it half to death. Later, I remember shuddering, seeing him look like some East End spiv, dripping in gold. There was my chain, and sovereign rings, and chunky gold bracelets, all topped off with a white leather jacket. I had never known how to describe this man to anyone, let alone my staff. I'd re-invented myself, I suppose. I'm not ashamed of that. I've never tried to pretend anything else. All I knew was that I didn't want to be like him, and any time I came even close to doing so, I would put the fear of God into myself. My father was in some box that, metaphorically speaking, I'd hidden in a dusty corner of the attic years ago.

And then there was my fear of being used. A while before he came back to England, during a busy service at Aubergine, someone came to me saying I had a phone call from my brother-in-law. At the time, I didn't have a brother-in-law.

'Dave, here,' said the voice.

'Look, Dave,' I said. 'I'm fucking busy right now. I haven't got time for pranks. You can call me back at fucking midnight.'

But he persisted. He refused to get off the line.

'Look, Dave,' I said, again. 'I don't know who the fuck you are but this is not the right fucking time. I'm not fucking happy.'

'Well, I don't care where you are or what you're cooking,' said the voice. 'My Mum is married to your dad.'

Then it clicked. That, you see, was how little I thought of Dad, and how little I knew about his new life. The voice said: 'I read that you do consultancy work for Singapore Airlines and my watch is from Singapore, and I can't get a battery in this country. Is there any chance you could get one for me next time you are out there?'

Perhaps you can imagine how I felt.

'Are you taking the fucking piss?' I said.

I put down the phone. Some guy I'd never even met ringing me in the middle of service to ask me to get him a new battery for his watch. I simply could not believe it.

It was New Year's Eve when we heard that my father died. The family were all in London, staying with me and Tana. It must have been about 3.30 a.m. We'd been in bed for an hour. Then the phone rang. I woke up and answered it and all I could hear was screaming. At first, I thought someone was trying to wish me a Happy New Year, but this person was in hysterics. She kept going on about some drug, how it hadn't worked. She kept going on about someone called Ricky Scott. I put down the phone. Then, as it began to sink in, I called this person back. It was Anne, and 'Ricky Scott' was Dad. Apparently, he'd changed his name. Scott was his mother's maiden name.

It was his alcoholism that had killed him. Of course, I drove straight down there, to the hospital. I felt fucking robotic. I was just going through the motions. That was the first time I had ever laid eyes on Anne. 'Oh my God,' she gasped. 'You're so like your father.' All I remember is lots of people smoking, and drinking tea. I was asked if I wanted to see him – Dad. I said no.

'I can't believe you're not going to see him,' she said.

'Well, that's my choice,' I said. I knew I wouldn't be very good at seeing a dead person. It just wasn't something I could put myself through. Years later, a close friend of mine died. I was asked to go and identify the body. But I couldn't. I had to send someone else. I wasn't any stronger then.

For all that I hated him, burying Dad was one of the worst days of my life. The funeral was horrible. She organised it, Anne, in a Margate crematorium so characterless it might as well have been a branch of Tesco. Oh, it was bad, really bad. We walked in, and his songs were playing, him singing. To me, that was the worst thing. And then, all these strangers . . . We knew no one.

Mum didn't go, but my sisters did. And Ronnie, though not without a fight. By this time, Ronnie was a desperate heroin addict, and he was refusing to go. I was at my wits' end. Finally, about an hour before the funeral, I gave him money so that he could buy what he needed to get him through. I thought it was better for him to be there and off his face, than not there at all. How low can you go? Very low indeed, if you're desperate.

We carried Dad in, in his wooden box, and I could have cried. I started listening to the service, and they were calling him Ricky. That wasn't even his name. His name's Gordon, I thought. Why the fuck are they calling him Ricky? Then Anne turned round, and said: 'I think your father would have wanted you to say a few words.' So I did.

'On behalf of the Ramsay family, I just want to say that we don't know this "Ricky". Dad's name is Gordon.' I got so upset I couldn't even finish my sentence. I burst into tears. It took me several attempts to get the words out. Afterwards, we tried to be polite. We went and spent the requisite fifteen minutes at the knees-up that she'd organised. But I couldn't have taken any more than that. Ronnie was out of it in any case. We could have been at a family christening for all he knew.

After that, I drove back to London and I went straight back to the kitchen. I was there, on the pass, working as hard as ever, trying not to think – or at least, to think only about the next order. I don't think I've ever needed my kitchen so much in all my life.

What did my father leave me? A watch, actually. Everything else he 'owned' was on hire purchase anyway. He never tasted my cooking in the end, though even if he had, I doubt he would have been impressed. 'Cooking is for poofs,' he used to say. 'Only poofs cook.'

But there is something else, too. Someone, I should say. Dad had another child, a girl, before he met Mum. Her parents adopted the baby. Apparently, Dad had planned on marrying her, but her parents had other ideas. One night, they went to see him sing, and then they followed him home and told him to stay away from their daughter. They threatened to beat him up. Perhaps his performance that evening had been even worse than usual. So that was that. He walked away, and went after Mum instead. My father's parents knew all about this child, but they kept it from Mum, though she found out, of course – and several times, when she was expecting Diane, she even saw his child.

CHAPTER TWO
FOOTBALL

I MUST HAVE been about eight when I realised I was good at football. It was football, not cooking, that was my first real passion. I was a left-footed player – still am – and I was always in the back garden, or out in the close, kicking a ball against the wall. I used to long for Saturday mornings. The night before, I'd polish my boots until I got the most amazing shine on them. I remember my first pair of football boots. They were second-hand, bought from the Barras by Mum, and they didn't fit properly; I had to wear two or three pairs of socks with them at first. But that didn't matter to me, because owning them was more exciting than anything.

Football was one way I thought I could impress Dad. Nothing else worked. He never came into school, to see how we were doing, and he never thought our swimming was as good as his. But he and my Uncle Ronald were huge Rangers fans, and I could see that this might be a way to reach him. Uncle Ronald had a season ticket, and any time we went up to Glasgow, we would go off to Ibrox to see a game. I must have been about seven when I went to my first match. I remember being up on Ronald's shoulders, and the incredible roar of the crowd. It was quite frightening. They still had the terraces in those days, and when the crowd celebrated, everyone surged forward: this great, heaving mass. I was always worried things might kick off, especially during derby matches. There was so much aggression between Rangers and Celtic and I could never understand why they had to be that nasty. My uncle told me that the men all worked together in the shipyard Monday to Friday but when it came to the weekend, they hated one another's guts. I was very struck by that as a boy.

Back in Stratford, I was chosen to play under-14 football when I was just eleven, and, later, I used to be excused from rugby and athletics because I was representing the county at football; at twelve years old, I played for War-wickshire. So I had a fair idea that other people thought I was good, too. Did I enjoy it? Well, it was certainly better than rugby, which I hated. I was skinny, really skinny, and whenever we played rugby I just used to get mullered. And yes, of course I enjoyed it. I loved it. But if I am honest, it was also a good way of getting out of the house, especially at weekends. If Dad came to watch it was a special relief because at least that meant he wasn't at home playing country and western, deafening all the neighbours, and giving Mum a hard time. He didn't always come to watch, though. On those days, you'd come home and Dickie Davies would be on the telly, and while you desperately tried to watch the results, Dad would be busy trying to prove to you that he was a better guitarist than Hank Marvin. Sometimes, he didn't even ask you the score, or whether or not you'd made any goals. I got used to it.

I had plenty of setbacks along the way, though, my progress was hardly meteoric. For one thing, we moved so often that I always had to secure a place in a new team. Then, when I was fourteen, I had the most terrible footballing accident. I was playing in a county match, in Leamington Spa. In the first two minutes of the game I went up to head a ball, and the miracle was that the ball went straight into the back of the net. Unfortunately, along the way, the goalkeeper had managed to punch me in the stomach and the combination of my exuberance and his mistaking the height of my jump meant that he somehow perforated my spleen. What a nightmare.

I went down and, at first, I thought I was only winded. The referee came over and sat me up and made me do all these sit-ups. I felt dizzy and weird. So he sent me off to get some water. I went to pee and suddenly I was peeing blood, and two minutes later I collapsed. An ambulance was called.

In the hospital, they didn't know it was my spleen. First,

they thought it was my appendix; then they thought it was a collapsed lung. That night, I was doubled over in pain. I was crippled with it and was crying my eyes out. The immense fucking agony, you would not have believed it. The doctors didn't know what to do. Dad was away for some reason, in Texas, I think, and no one could get hold of Mum, so there was no one to sign the consent forms. In the end, they took me down to surgery anyway and somehow managed to repair the damage, though they took my appendix out as well, in the end. I was scared. I wanted Mum.

The operation really knocked me back. But there was worse to come. Two weeks later, an abscess developed internally. So it was back into hospital. This time, I had blood poisoning. All told, my recovery took three months from start to finish. I couldn't do anything physical. I couldn't run, I couldn't jump and I couldn't train. That was a terrible blow for a fourteen-year-old boy. And then when I started kicking the ball again, I was nervous about going into a tackle. I had lost my confidence.

If Dad had been there, at the hospital, if he'd understood how serious the situation had been, he might have been a bit more sympathetic. But he wasn't. When he eventually came back, he announced that he'd managed to get some construction work in Amsterdam, and that he was going to take me with him while I convalesced. I was really excited, but only for one reason. I wanted to go and look at the Ajax stadium. The trouble was, it was only about ten weeks since the operation, I still wasn't as well as I should have been, and Dad was hardly the kind of man to take care of me. For days, I was just left to wander round this stadium. We were in bed-and-breakfast accommodation, so he would go off to work (though that, predictably, lasted about three weeks), leaving me behind with four guilders to my name. You don't realise it till later – that you've been abandoned. I think now: fuck, I was on my jack, wandering around, a fourteen-year-old boy who's just had major surgery. It was fun, going to the Ajax stadium one, two, three times. But then – even the fucking gardeners got to know me. That was a very, very strange trip.

I had pictures of my heroes, Kenny Dalglish and Kevin Keegan, on my bedroom wall, but I never thought I'd be professional. Apart from anything, even after the accident, I still had terrible problems with my feet. I was cramming my feet into boots that were too small – the ethos of the day was to get boots that were a size too small. Even my coach told me to do that. Some Saturday nights, I'd sit on the side of the bath, wearing my boots, with my feet in hot water, trying to literally mould the leather around them. To this day, I've got toes that are bent at the end – hammer toes. By the time I'm an old man, they'll be like claws. I never had the money for decent boots, even if they'd been the right size. I had to make them last and then, when they were finally worn out, when they looked like a few bits of old cardboard tied together with string, Mum had to secretly slip me money to buy a new pair.

When we moved down to Banbury, I began playing for Banbury United. I suppose that's when I started getting noticed, though I was only paid my expenses because I was still at school. I played left back. Every term, players from our team were invited up to Oxford United, where they trained with the third or fourth team, and then played for the reserve side, which meant that they got to spend the most amazing week up there. I was picked up by coach and taken there – the first time that I'd been made to feel special, or any good at all, really. And then the travelling became more of a regular event – though I was crap at that. The coach used to make me feel so ill. A small bowl of porridge for breakfast and then, an hour later, I'd be sick as a dog. Hardly the hard man.

I remember my first serious game like it was yesterday. Dad was away and I couldn't take Mum because, well, you don't take your mum to football, do you? It was an English Schools competition, Oxfordshire County vs Inner London, and it was to be held at Loftus Road, the ground of Queens Park Rangers, in London. Amazing. A big, fucking stadium instead of the cow patch we had to play on in Banbury, and all the London players were from the youth teams of Chelsea, Tottenham and Arsenal. I thought we were going to get absolutely hammered – that the score would be 8–0 or something. These guys were bigger and stronger than us.

48

But the funny thing was that we beat them 2–1. But it was a dirty game. I was taken off, fifteen minutes before the end of the second half, after a bad tackle to my knee. Another injury from which it took me ages to recover. Perhaps I was doomed when it came to football.

After I'd recovered, I played in an FA Cup youth game and it was there that a Rangers scout spotted me. They asked if I'd like to spend a week of my next summer holiday with the club. Fucking hell. I couldn't believe it. It wasn't just the fact that it was a professional club; it was RANGERS, the one that would really have an impact on the way Dad felt about me – or so I thought. The trouble was, Mum and Dad were going through a really shitty time then, and in a way, it put me under even more pressure. A part of me didn't want anyone to know, just in case I couldn't pull it off. I didn't want to let anyone down and, in doing so, unwittingly make things even worse between them. By this point, I was sixteen and was pushing the upper age limit as far as breaking into professional football went. It was make-or-break time.

That first week was hard. I didn't have a good time at all. I had an English accent, for one thing, so basically they just kicked the shit out of me for that. And they also made me use my right leg, which was fucking useless. We weren't allowed to rely on only one foot, in much the same way as, in the kitchen, you must be able to chop with both hands. I'm naturally left-handed, but I can chop and peel with my right hand so if I cut myself, I'm okay – I'm prepared. Anyway, after that first week, I came back and I just hated Rangers. I hated the guts out of them. I had no problem with the training – I've never been afraid of hard work – but then, in the afternoons, after training, we had gone on to play snooker and eat for Britain. Food in Scotland was bad, then – unbelievably bad. It still is, in most cases. It was pie and gravy, pie and beans, or what the Scottish call a 'slice' – these big, square, processed slabs of sausage meat. Fucking hell. I didn't have what you'd call a sophisticated palate, but I couldn't stand it. And although I was in digs, with the other lads, I was very lonely. I wished I had a Scottish accent, something that would have made them feel more comfortable around me.

'I was born in Johnstone, and Mum and Dad moved south,' I kept trying to tell them. 'But my gran and my uncle and aunt all live in Port Glasgow.'

They, of course, weren't having any of it.

I suppose after that first week up there, I thought I'd really fucked it up. I was called back three times. The process was horrible, and I was in two minds about begging for a fucking contract out of Rangers. I was settled in Banbury in the flat with Diane and I'd started a foundation course in catering and it was going well, and there was this feeling, deep inside me, that something else was bubbling up. I was starting to get excited about food. Also, though Mum and Dad's relationship was really going pear-shaped, they had moved back up to Scotland, and I was enjoying my freedom. I had my first serious girlfriend, I'd started working in a local hotel, I had a bit of money, and there was always Banbury United if I wanted football. I got about £15 a game. I wasn't complaining. Still, I was just waiting for that call.

Mum phoned. She told me to contact my Uncle Ronald: he had some good news for me about Rangers. So that was what I did. 'Look, things have moved on,' he said. 'I told you they were going to watch you, and they have, and they're going to invite you back up.'

He gave me a number to call. It was for one of the head coaches. I couldn't understand a word he was saying: he was speaking far, far too fast. But finally he said: 'We want you back up. Can you bring your Dad to training on May seventeenth?'

I thought: oh, shit. At that point, I was barely speaking to Dad. I wasn't even allowed to call the house. The trouble was that the first people the club want to talk to are your parents. They want to know that you've got security at home, that you're properly supported. I was thinking: fuck, am I properly supported? No. I'm sixteen, and I'm living on my own, fending for myself. I rang Mum and asked her to tell him. I couldn't face doing it myself.

So she did tell him and, all of a sudden he was . . . I don't know. Not nice, exactly, but smarmy. He was excited now. I guess he had his eye on the main chance. He was going to live vicariously, through me. How did I feel about this? Wary and nervous. I knew he was drinking; I knew he'd been horrible to Mum; I knew what Yvonne had been through. The only thing that kept me going was the fact that Dad had promised to buy Mum a house – the first time he'd ever suggested such a thing. I hung on to that promise for dear life. I picked up on that one tiny moment, and managed to convince myself that he must have got his shit together at last. Still, it all felt so false – everyone pretending to be best mates, Dad and my uncle suddenly being so involved in my life. I had to live at home again, and take Dad to training with me every day. Being back there, I knew that things weren't at all right. I felt it instantly. It was almost like Mum and Dad were staying together for the sake of my future at Rangers. I couldn't bear that. It was pressure, massive pressure. It wasn't as though I was in love with Dad and he had this amazing relationship with Mum, and all I had to do was concentrate and play football. I was worried. It was all so precarious – a house of cards that could tumble down around my ears at any moment.

This time, the training was going exceptionally well. I started playing in the testimonial games, and I was included on the first-team sheet, which was amazing. It was great, turning up to meet the bus when we were playing away from Ibrox, standing there waiting in your badge and tie, all spruced and immaculate as if you were off to a wedding. It was such a thrill. Outside the stadium, you'd be signing things like pillow cases and the side of prams, and families would turn up with their kids to have their trainers signed. Of course, they didn't know me from Adam. They didn't have a clue who I was. I was never a famous Rangers player because I was a member of the youth team. But, on the other hand, I was part of a squad that was doing well. The team has such a following that if you're wearing the gear – you're in, and that's that.

I played for the first team twice, but only in friendlies, or pre-season. In those days, Ally McCoist had just broken into the first-team squad – we still know one another now, though for different reasons, which is really weird – and Derek Ferguson was captain of the under-21s. But it was a bad time for me, stars or no stars. Dad's duplicity was really getting to me. Then they said: 'We're going to continue watching you. We're really excited. We are going to sign you – but it'll be next year rather than this.' Well, that was tough. I knew I was going to go back – how could I not – but by this time, I'd been offered a cooking job in London. Somewhere, I've still got the letter offering it to me. It was a new 300-seater banqueting hall that had opened at the Mayfair Hotel called The Crystal Room. They were looking for four commis chefs: second commis, grade two. I don't know what the fuck that means, even now – it's a posh kitchen porter, basically. But the salary was £5,200 a year. Anyway, I told them that I wasn't available to start and went back up to Rangers for the third year in a row.

This must have been the summer of 1984. Half the players weren't there because they were travelling in Canada, so everything was much more focused on the youth players. Basically, they were deciding who was staying, who they were going to sign that year. Coisty was there, and Derek and Ian Ferguson, whose contracts were well under way. They'd been involved with the club since they were boys, and I suppose that's all I ever really wanted to do, too: to stay put in one place, and play football, and become a local boy.

But if you're trying to make it in one of the best teams in Europe, and you don't even sound Scottish, you're like a huge, fucking foreigner. Luckily, I was getting big and strong and I could just about handle myself. The training went very well, this time. I remember playing in a reserve team game against Coisty. They always used to hold back two or three first-team players, and then they'd give the inside track about what you were like on the pitch. I had a good game. I was hopeful. I was feeling positive.

The following week, we were playing a massive testimonial in East Kilbride. I couldn't believe it. I was in the squad, and I got to play. There must have been about 9,000 supporters at the game. The trouble was that they kept moving me around the pitch, playing me out of position. First I was centre back. Then I played centre mid-field, where you've got to have two equally strong feet, and you have to be able to twist and turn suddenly. I was really pissed off, and then, just to make things even worse, I got taken off fifteen minutes before the end. They must have made at least seven different substitutions that day. Never mind. I trained for another two weeks, and then I played in another youth team match. Another really, really good game. I was starting to think that I might be in with a chance.

Then, disaster. The pity of it is that my football career effectively came to an end in a training session – one of those bizarre training accidents where you barely realise what it is that you have done. I smashed my cartilage, seriously damaging my knee, and stupidly, I tried to play on. There had been one of those horrendous tackles that makes you even more determined not to give up. I would do whatever I was asked to do, no question. We went on to take penalties with our right foot. I'll never forget it. We had to put a trainer on our left foot and a football boot on our right. The idea was to make your right foot work constantly. So first there was a penalty competition and then, afterwards, we had to take corners with our right foot. It must have been nearly four o'clock when they finally said, right, we're going to divide into two teams of eleven and play fifteen minutes each way and I want you all to give it everything you've fucking got. By this time, we'd been training all day. Well, that was a big mistake. By the time we finished, I was in a serious amount of pain.

Afterwards, I should still have been resting up, but I tried to get back into the game too quickly. I was out for eleven long weeks, getting more and more paranoid, terrified that someone else would take my place on the bench. But no sooner was I up and running again than I played a game of squash. That was a really dumb thing to do. I tore a cruciate ligament during the game, and was in plaster for another four months. I was worried that I wouldn't regain my match fitness. Once the plaster came off, I started training again like a demon. But I was still in a lot of pain, though I tried to ignore it. After training sessions, I would spend hours in hot and cold baths, trying to ease the pain, to reduce any swelling. Deep down, I think I knew I was in trouble, but I pushed those kinds of thoughts to the back of my mind. I would tell myself: maybe all players are in this much pain. Or: maybe I can work through it. I was determined to put in a third appearance for the first team, and in order to do that, I had to ignore the message my body was trying to send me.

But come the start of the new season, there was no getting away from it. My leg was just not the same, and this had become apparent to my bosses. Jock Wallace, the club's manager, and his assistant, Archie Knox, called me into their office one Friday morning to give me the bad news. It was all over for me. I was not going to be signed. I was not going to play European, or even first division football. I remember their words coming at me like physical blows. It was so hard to take. But I was determined not to show how broken I felt inside. Years of standing up to Dad had put me in good stead for this performance. I might have wanted to cry, or to shout, or to punch the nearest wall, but I was damned if I was going to in front of these two. I admired Jock and I had always been intimidated by him. I certainly wasn't going to let the side down now. I gripped my chair, and waited for the whole thing to be over. In those few minutes, all my dreams died. Part of me was wondering how I would manage to walk out of the room.

They suggested I do more physio, and maybe sign with a different club, one in a lower league. So did my father. In fact, he was pathetically eager that I take this advice. I don't think he could bear to lose sight of the dreams he had had for me. He wanted the good times to roll. He wanted to be able to boast to his so-called friends, who had always been so much more of a success in life than him. Dad was sitting in his van just outside the ground when Wallace broke the news to me; going out there and telling him was one of the toughest things I have ever done. But I wouldn't let him have the pleasure of seeing me cry, either. On and on he went: 'You carry on badgering Rangers,' he said. 'You prove to them you are fit again.' But far harder to take was his lack of sympathy for me. He didn't have a single kind word for me that day, not even so much as a gentle pat on the shoulder. Later on, he even suggested that I might be exaggerating the extent of my injury. So I went home, shut myself away, and had a good cry. I couldn't face seeing anyone. I suppose I mourned for what might have been. But I was also certain that I had no future in football. Scrabbling around playing games here and there and working some other day job to pay the bills wasn't for me. I wanted it all, or I wanted nothing. No matter how much promise I had shown, I was always going to be labelled as the player with the gammy knee. I had to let go of the game that I loved. That was hard because I had come so close to making it, and I felt bitter for a long, long time afterwards. But I was certain that I was doing the right thing in making a clean break: I had the example of my father and his so-called music career to encourage me, didn't I? There was no way I wanted to be a pathetic dreamer like him for the rest of my life. The very idea disgusted me. I wanted to be the best at whatever I did, not the kind of guy that people secretly laughed at behind his back. I needed a new challenge. The only question was: what would that be?

Looking back on this time, I'm struck, once again, by the cruelty of my father, and the way he dominated everything I did, even my football. I loved the game. But my involvement wasn't about becoming a famous player with flash cars and flash houses and women hanging on my every word. It had so much more to do with proving myself to my father. I remember one night, when he was very drunk, he said to me that he used to think that I was gay when I was a little boy. I will never forget that. What is striking to me about that now is that he was so full of hatred for the idea that I might be gay; I couldn't help but wonder why the idea made him feel so threatened. What was his problem?

The film *Billy Elliot* has an amazing resonance for me. I remember going to see the musical version of it on stage in London with Tana. Fucking amazing. There was a moment – you can probably guess which one – when it took me straight back to my bedroom, to Dad being furious with me and accusing me of being gay. It moved me so much that I could hardly swallow for twenty-four hours. I know that world, where things are so hard. Mum trying to bake bread because we hadn't even enough money to buy a loaf; us all depending on fucking powdered Marvel milk for months and months on end. No wonder I was so fucking thin. You never forget all that, and when you see the same kind of life up there on the big screen, you have one flashback after another. Not to be self-pitying, but it can leave you in pieces.

Of course, going into cooking probably got Dad thinking all that crap about my being gay all over again. He always thought that any man who cooked had to be gay – and he wasn't alone. When I started out, this country had no culture of great kitchens. It wasn't like France – cooking was a suspect profession for a man. You may as well have said that you wanted to be a hairdresser.

When I first started working in a kitchen, I kept the two worlds – football and food – as far apart as I could. One night, when I was at Harvey's, Coisty came in for dinner with Terry Venables. I didn't say a word to anyone. I didn't want the other cooks to know about my life at Rangers, and I didn't want anyone connected with football to see me in my whites. It seems bloody silly now. But back then, it felt like a matter of life and death. What a long way I have come.

CHAPTER THREE

GETTING STARTED

Growing up, there wasn't a lot of money for food. But we never went hungry. Mum was a good, simple cook: ham hock soup, bread and butter pudding, and fish fingers, homemade chips and beans. We had one of those ancient chip pans with a mesh basket inside it, and oil that got changed about once a decade. I loved it that the chips were all different sizes. She used to do liver for Dad – that was the only thing I refused to eat – and tripe in milk and onions; the smell of it used to linger around the house for days and days. Steak was a rarity: sausages and chops were all we could afford. We were poor, and there was no getting away from it. Lunch was dinner, and dinner was tea, and the idea of having a starter, main course and pudding was unimaginable. Did people really do that? If we were shopping in the Barras, and we decided to have a fish supper, we children all had to share. There was no way we would each be allowed to order for ourselves. Later on, when Mum had a job in a little tea shop in Stratford, she'd bring home stuff that hadn't been sold. We regarded these as the most unbelievable treats: steak-and-kidney pies and chocolate éclairs.

We were permanently on free school dinners. That was terrible. It used to make me cringe. In our first few years, of course, none of the other kids quite cottoned on to what those vouchers were about. But higher up the school it became fucking embarrassing. They'd tease you, try to kick the shit out of you. On the last Friday of every month, the staff made a point of calling out your name to give you the next month's tickets. That was hell. It was pretty much confirmation that you were one of the poorest kids in the class. If they'd tattooed this information on your forehead, it couldn't have been any clearer. So yes, I did associate plentiful food with good times, with status. But I'd be lying if I said I was interested in cooking. As a boy, it was just another chore. My career came about pretty much by mistake.

I latched on to the idea of catering college because my options were limited, to say the least. I didn't know if the football would work out. I looked at the Navy and at the Police, but I didn't have enough O levels to join either of them. As for the Marines, my little brother, Ronnie, was joining the Army, and I couldn't face the idea of competing with him. So I ended up enrolling on a foundation year in catering at a local college, sponsored by the Rotarians. It was an accident, a complete accident. Did I dream of being a Michelin-starred chef? Did I fuck! The very first thing I learned to do? A béchamel sauce. You got your onion, and you studded it with cloves. Then you got your bay leaves. Then you melted your butter and added some flour to it to make a roux. And no, I don't bloody make it that way any more. I remember coming home and showing Diane how to chop an onion really finely. I had my own wallet of knives, a kind that came with plastic banana-yellow handles. At *Royal Hospital Road*, we wouldn't even use those to clean the shit off a non-stick pan, let alone chop with them. But we were so proud of them – and of our chef's whites. I treated my knives and my whites with exactly the same love and reverence as I used to my football boots. I sent a picture of me in my big, white chef's hat up to Mum in Glasgow. I think she still has it. I was so fucking proud.

Meanwhile, I had a couple of weekend jobs. The first was in a curry house in Stratford – washing up. The kitchen there wasn't the cleanest place in the world, and they worked me into the ground. Then, in Banbury, Diane got me a job working in the hotel where she was a waitress. Again, I was only washing up, but that was when I first got the idea of becoming a chef. I was in the kitchen, listening to all the noise, and I was fascinated. I couldn't believe the way people were shouting at each other. I was working like a fucking donkey, but the time used to fly by. I was enraptured.

After a year, one of my tutors suggested to me that I start working full-time, and attend college only on a day-release basis. I'd made good progress. That said, I was by no means the best kid in the class. In college, you can spot the students from the council estate, the ones who are basically middle-class, and the ones whose parents are so in love with their daughters that they send them to cookery school. God knows why. There are three tiers, and you can spot them a mile off. I was in the first group. I didn't get distinctions, and I wasn't Student of the Year. But I did keep my head down, and I did work my bollocks off. I pushed myself beyond belief. I was happy to learn the basics. I didn't find it demeaning at all.

So I started work as a commis at the place where I'd been washing up: the Roxburgh House Hotel. The dining room was pink – pink walls, pink linen – all the waiters were French and Italian and all the cooks were English. My first chef was this twenty-stone, bald guy called Andy Rogers. He was an absolute shire horse. The kind of guy who would tell you off without ever explaining why. Dear God, the kind of food that he encouraged us to turn out. I shudder to think of it. The cooking was shocking, the menus hilarious. Take the roast potatoes. They started off in the deep fat fryer and then they were sprinkled with Bisto granules before they went in the oven, to make sure they were nice and brown. Extraordinary. The foie gras was all tinned.

We used to serve mushrooms stuffed with Camembert.

One of the dishes was called a scallop of veal cordon bleu. It was basically a piece of battered veal wrapped around a ball of grated Gruyère in ham. I knew it was all atrocious, even then. I was getting all this information at college, and I would come back and try to apply it. I'd say: 'You know there's a short cut. To make fish stock you should only cook it for twenty minutes, otherwise it will get cloudy, and then you should let it rest before you pass it through a sieve, or it will go cloudy again.' For this, I would get roundly bollocked by the chef. He didn't give a fuck for college.

I stayed for about six months, and then I got a job at a really good place called the Wickham Arms, in a small village in Oxfordshire. The owners were Paul and Jackie, and the idea was that I would live above the shop, which was a beautiful thatched cottage. Unfortunately, things went pear-shaped there pretty early on. Jackie was in her thirties, I must have been about nineteen, Paul was away a lot; perhaps you can imagine what was going to happen.

Paul was mad about golf, and he loved his real ale. So he'd be off down to Cornwall, in search of these wonderful kegs. I had a serious girlfriend at the time, I'd met her at the college but she was going off to university. So that didn't stop me. Basically, I was in charge of the kitchen, and a 60-seat dining room, and I wasn't even properly qualified yet. I was making dishes like jugged hare and venison casserole and doing these amazing pâtés, and just reading endless numbers of cookery books. Locally, everyone loved

67

the food, and it became a kind of hot spot. But I guess that went to my head: I was on my own, completely free, no one checking up on me. I was all over the fucking shop.

One day, while Paul was off on one of his trips, Jackie rang down to the kitchen. 'Can I have something to eat?' she said.

'What would you like?'

'Just bring me a simple salad, thanks.'

So I got together a salad with a little poached salmon and took it up.

'Jackie, your dinner is ready.'

And she opened the door – stark bollock naked. I put the tray down, and went straight into her bedroom.

For the next six months, I led a kind of double life. There was Jackie, my teacher, and Helen, my pupil. You know what it's like when you're young. It's awkward and clumsy. Sometimes, at least before I met Jackie, I used to feel that sex was like sharpening a pencil. You stick it in there, and grind it around. But Jackie was teaching me all these things, and it was amazing. The trouble was that Helen got some of the fringe benefits, which meant that she was falling more and more in love with me.

At first, Paul would only be away for a couple of days at a time. Then he started going on golfing trips to Spain for more like a week. That's when it all got too much. It was getting heavy. Fucking heavy. Jackie told me that she loved me. The truth is that I loved making the jugged hare more than I did having sex with the boss's wife, but the only reason I was in a position to buy and cook exactly what I wanted was precisely because I was shagging her. Things weren't exactly going to plan and it was all getting too nerve-racking for me: that he might notice, that we might get caught, the fact that she was always telling me she was in love with me. So I told them that I was leaving to go and work in London. She went bananas.

I actually went back to the Wickham Arms two years later, for a mate's twenty-first. Someone must have told Paul because, while she was still being very flirtatious, he was clearly not too pleased to see me. I was in the kitchen, talking to the new chef, telling him how good I thought the buffet was. There was a carrot cake sitting there and, without thinking, I stuck my finger in it. Well, one of the waitresses must have snitched on me to Paul because a split second later, he came running in and shoved me hard against the wall.

'I should have fucking done this three years ago,' he said. 'You know what the fuck I'm on about.'

He then took a swing at me, but fortunately one of my mates intervened, which gave me enough time to make a very sharp exit. So I ran from the kitchen, jumped in the car and disappeared into the night. Hilarious. The next time I saw them was quite a long time later, when they turned up at Aubergine in the early part of 1998. They'd opened a new restaurant in a village in Buckinghamshire, and they brought their chef to meet me at Aubergine. By then, a lot of water had passed under the bridge. They had rung me, told me that he was a big fan of mine, and asked if they could come by. I said, sure, of course. It was embarrassing – I mean, I'd moved on, I wasn't just poaching salmon and chopping aspic any more – but I made out it was good to see them all. The trouble was, they got pissed and a bit leery and then, when they missed the train back to Buckinghamshire, they started demanding that I offer them a bed for the night. We did try to ring around and find them a room, but hotels were £250 per night, which seem to make them even more aggrieved. I don't know what they expected me to do – ask them back to sleep on the floor of my flat as well as cook their food? Well, I wasn't having that. Tana was pregnant at the time, so I sent out their dessert and then I fucked off.

At half-past one in the morning, I got a call from Jean-Claude, my maître d'. He was screaming at me down the telephone. This chef of theirs was holding him over the bar, demanding that the arrogant fucker who left without saying goodbye – i.e. me – come on the line. About fifty minutes later, I rocked up on my motorbike. I thought I better had, and I was right. It was total mayhem. There was Mark, my head chef, fighting with Paul, and Paul's new chef fighting with Jean-Claude. Naturally, I just could not stand by and watch Aubergine get trashed or my staff take a beating. But they both moved towards me before I had time to think. Paul was going: 'I trusted you. How dare you – you shagged my wife!' All my staff were thinking: WHAT? I could see it on their faces. The resulting mêlée caused major headlines when the Old Bill arrived because there was so much blood everywhere. We all got taken off to make statements and then, when the whole thing was written up in the London *Evening Standard*, predictably, it was me who was supposed to have thrown all of the punches. It was all: 'I came to meet the great master and instead found an arrogant bastard', 'Brawl that wasn't on the menu' and 'Ramsay punched my husband in the mouth'. That kind of rubbish. I had to take legal action to clear that one up. I kept my powder dry until all the other papers had followed suit and then I issued proceedings. I won, of course. As for Paul, he sobered up pretty fast once he got back to Buckinghamshire. He sent me a fax apologising. That was the end of that.

To be fair, they really looked after me, those two. Before it all went wrong. I mean, I wasn't exactly as sweet as pie. Of course I wasn't Mr Innocent. I was a little fucker, actually – no mum and dad around, a place to live, a girl-friend, thinking I was the dog's bollocks. I would borrow my girlfriend's father's car all the time, even though I hadn't passed my test. I used to leave the kitchen at half-past one in the morning and drive down the country lanes, over to Helen's. One night, I left the pub in this car, and turned a corner only to be met by two sets of headlights:

one car overtaking another on a bend. I pulled out of the way, but they hit the back of my car and it went into a spin, straight into the very prettily beamed sitting room of the nearest cottage. My head was cut, my knees were cut and all I wanted to do was to make myself scarce as quickly as possible because, of course, I shouldn't have been driving at all. My test was still five weeks away. So that's what I did – I absconded. Unfortunately, the police picked me up three hours later, hiding out in some fucking manure dump.

Naturally, I was prosecuted. As it turned out, the case came up the day after I was due to take my test. My solicitor told me that he strongly advised me to pass it because it would help my case in court, but I failed and so, in the end, I was banned for a year even though officially I wasn't actually able to drive. I was also fined £400. About five years ago, I got a solicitor's letter from the new owners of the cottage I'd smashed up; they were still trying to claim the £27,000 worth of damage I caused. Pass the place today and, in the spot where I made my unannounced house call, you can see that the bricks are still two different colours. Yes, I might have been an extremely ambitious young man, but I was also a bit of a tearaway. I can't deny it. I don't really blame Paul for wanting to beat me up. Any man would have done the same in his position.

*   *   *

So, to the starry lights of London. I was second commis, grade two, at the Mayfair Hotel, in its new banqueting rooms, as planned. I stayed about sixteen months, and I learned a lot. I used to make the most amazing sandwiches, the smoked salmon sliced incredibly thinly, because I had to do room service as well. On my day off, I would work overtime without getting paid, just for the chance to work in what we used to call the Château – the hotel's fine-dining restaurant, where all the staff was French. If you fucked up during service, you had to work in the hotel coffee shop. That was the punishment. It was a tough place. If someone called in sick, you could easily end up working a twenty-four-hour shift. You'd work all day in the restaurant, and then during the night you'd man the grill and do the room service. At half-past four in the morning, all the Indian kitchen boys would sit down and have their supper, and then they'd go and pray for an hour, and you'd already be doing prep for the next morning's breakfast. In those days, a hotel's scrambled eggs were done in a bain-marie. You whipped up three trays of eggs and then you put them, along with some cream and seasoning, into the bain-marie so it could cook slowly, over a period of two and a half hours, at the end of which it was like fucking rubber.

Naturally, like a true goody two-shoes, I said: 'Look, I'm on breakfasts this morning. I'm going to make all the scrambled eggs to order, chef.' And that's exactly what I did, though I got fucked when I came back from my day off because there'd been so many complaints about how slow the breakfasts had been. 'But chef,' I said. 'I may have been a bit slow, but at least they weren't rubber eggs. They were freshly made to order.' He wasn't having any of it. 'I don't give a fuck,' he said. 'We had to knock about twenty-five breakfasts off bills.' I got such a bollocking – a written warning, in fact. But when he gave it to me, in a funny way, it was helpful. It was there in black and white that I was working in a place that wasn't for me – a place where you got a warning for failing to cook crap scrambled eggs. I knew I had to get out.

In those days, there was a really cool restaurant called Maxine de Paris, just off Leicester Square, and I'd heard that they were opening a new restaurant in Soho called Braganza. So I got a job there as a sort of third commis chef, though I didn't stay long because all the food went in a dumb waiter, rather than being picked up straight off the pass by a human being, which meant it was always a bit cold, and I just couldn't come to terms with that. But there was an amazing sous chef there called Martin Dickinson – now the head chef at J. Sheekey – who'd worked at a restaurant called Waltons in Walton Street, a Michelin-starred place, and he was just phenomenal. I suppose that's when I started thinking that Michelin stars were the Holy Grail, and that I wanted to work in a serious restaurant. Because Martin seemed like a God to me.

'Get yourself into a decent kitchen,' he told me. 'This

place isn't for you. Trust me, you don't want to be working in a place that serves smoked chicken and papaya salad. Get the fuck out of here.'

I would have worked it out somewhere down the line, but I owe it to Martin that I moved so quickly. I went up to the staff canteen, which was just a grotty little room, really, where all the chefs would smoke, and I grabbed a magazine and I took it out into the garden in Soho Square. 'Christ,' I said to myself. 'There's Jesus.' Because on its cover was a photograph of Marco Pierre White, all long hair and bruised-looking eyes. I was nineteen. He was twenty-five. He'd come from a council estate in Leeds and then, when I looked at who he'd worked with and where . . . Nico Ladenis, Raymond Blanc, La Tante Claire and Le Gavroche. I thought: fuck me, he's worked for all the best chefs in Britain. I want to go and work with him.

I phoned him up then and there.

'Where are you working now?' he said. So I told him.

'Well, it must be a fucking shit hole because Alastair Little is the only place that I know in Soho, and if you're not working there then don't bother coming.'

I wasn't sure what to say to that, so I told him, without even really thinking about it, that I was about to go to France because I wanted to learn how to cook properly.

'Have you got a job out there?' he asked.

'No, not yet.'

'Then come and see me tomorrow morning.'

I left the phone box and went back to the restaurant. I couldn't stop thinking about what he'd said.

I turned up at what would become the legendary Harvey's the following day, as requested. We're talking about the earliest days of the restaurant. It had only been open about six months, and it would be another six months before it got its first Michelin star.

I suppose I expected to walk in and see him sitting at a table writing menus or something. Not a bit of it. I walked into this dingy alleyway, and said to a guy who was standing there: 'Can I speak to Marco?' The guy turned round and looked at me. It was him.

'Are you Gordon?'

'Yeah.'

'Stand there.'

I did as I was told. I just stood there for about twenty minutes while he boned pigs' trotters. I didn't know what to think. Part of me wanted to go 'fuck this' and walk out, but another part of me was so fascinated by what he was doing that I stopped noticing how much time had passed.

Finally, he took me through to the dining room there, sat me down and gave me a coffee.

'Look,' he said. 'We work so fucking hard here. This kitchen will be your life. There's no social life, no girlfriends, and it's shit money. Do you want to leave now?'

'No, no. Not at all.'

So that was it. Next thing, he's telling me to get changed and come into the kitchen. He was making pasta. I'd never made pasta in my life. He showed me how to do a ravioli, he showed me how to do a tortellini, then I had a go.

'Those aren't going on the menu,' he said. 'They aren't perfect. But things are moving pretty quickly here.'

I was scared of fucking up. But it was almost like doing an assault course. No matter what happened, you had to finish that fucking course. So even if I was clumsy, I was determined to get there in the end.

'Your fingers move fast,' he said. 'Do you want a job?'

'Yeah, I'd love a job.'

'You start Monday.'

But Monday was going to be a problem. 'I've got to give a month's notice,' I said.

'Well, if you really want the job that fucking badly, you start Monday.'

I was shitting myself, but there was nothing for it: later on that day I phoned him and told him that the people at Braganza were refusing to pay me that month's salary unless I worked my notice.

'I've got this to pay and that to pay,' I said. 'I'm going to have to stay put.'

'What hours are you working?'

'I'm on earlies for the next month.'

Problem solved. I did the early shift at Braganza from 7 a.m. until 4 p.m., and then I got the tube to Victoria, and the train from there to Wandsworth Common, where I'd work at Harvey's until about two o'clock the following morning. I kept this up for the whole month. I had no choice. It turned out that Marco's warning about the restaurant taking over my life was only the half of it.

In the beginning, I admired Marco more than I can say. I wasn't in love with the mythology – you know, this screwed-up boy who'd lost his mother at six and had been dedicating dishes to her memory ever since – but his cooking left me speechless: the lightness, the control, the fact that everything was made to order. In the kitchen, there'd be six portions of beef, or sea bass, or tagliatelle, not fifty. Everything was so fresh, everything was made to order.

There was one dish I particularly admired – Marco's tagliatelle of oysters with caviar. In his most famous book, *White Heat*, he spouted all kinds of shit about that dish, about how it was his first 'perfect flower', how some chefs spend a lifetime looking for a dish like that. Bollocks. Still, I do believe that it will go down as a classic. The oysters had been poached in their own juices; the shells had twirls of tagliatelle in, and the oysters on top of that, and some wonderful thin strips of cucumber that had been poached in oyster juice, all topped with caviar. It was elegant, delicious and simple. It was extraordinary. Not that I ever got to eat it. We tasted, tasted, tasted, but we never actually ate. I never saw Marco sit down and eat. Never.

It was as if I was putting on my first pair of football boots all over again. I felt very low on the ladder. Speedwise, I was fine; my knife skills were great. But everything else I'd learned, I'd had to forget fast. Everything we produced had such great integrity: it was clean, honest food, and it tasted phenomenal. You'd taste a sauce ten, maybe fifteen times for a single portion. Then you'd start all over again when the next table's order came in. One portion, one sauce.

But it was the toughest place to work that you could imagine. You had to push yourself to the limit every day and every night. You had to learn to take a lot of shit, and to bite your lip and work even harder when that happened. A lot of the boys couldn't take the pace. They fell by the wayside. When that happened, you felt that you had been able to survive what they hadn't.

Marco was running a dictatorship: his word, and his word alone, was all that mattered. He fancied himself as a kind of Mafioso, dark and brooding and fucking terrifying. He had favourites, and then they would be out in the cold. He would praise you, and then he would knock you down. He would abuse you mentally and physically. He would appear when you were least expecting him, silently. His mood swings were unbelievable. One minute, he was all smiles, ruffling your hair, practically pinching your cheek.

The next he was throwing a pan across the kitchen. Often, the pan would be full. Stock everywhere, or boiling water, or soup. But you wouldn't say anything. You'd wait for the quiet after the storm, and then you'd clear up, no questions asked. Marco was never in the wrong. If you didn't like that, you were more than welcome to walk out of the door and take a job in some other restaurant. But he knew, and we knew, that there wasn't anywhere like Harvey's. There were better kitchens, with more stars and older reputations, but this place was something different. We were a tiny, young team, and we were blazing a trail. *White Heat*, with its arty black-and-white photos and its breathless fucking commentary, was well named.

The first time I saw Marco pummel a guy, I just stood there, my jaw swinging. It was a guy called Jason Everett. He got bollocked and I didn't know where to look. I mean it. He was physically beaten, on the floor. Another time, Egon Ronay was in the restaurant, and we had this veal dish on the menu. Well, Jason had overcooked all the kidneys. So Marco went bananas. 'Okay, Marco,' Jason said. 'I fucked the kidneys. I'll go and apologise to Egon Ronay. I'll go out there and apologise. Let me go. I've had enough.' He went out into the alleyway outside the restaurant and that's when Marco said: 'Those chef whites, those trousers, that's my fucking linen. You fucking take them off and walk round in your underpants.' So that's what the poor bastard did. He ripped off his whites and his trousers and he was bawling his eyes out, and then he had to walk past the front of the restaurant half naked.

We were all young and insecure, and he played on that. A lot of us were guys with a lot of baggage. He'd find out about your home life while you stood there peeling your asparagus or your baby potatoes. Then, four hours later, when you were in the middle of service and you'd screwed up, he would say: 'I fucking told you that you were a shit cook. You can't fucking roast a pigeon because you're too busy worrying about your mum and dad's divorce.' One time he turned round and said to me: 'You know the best thing that's happened to you, Ramsay? The shit that ran down your mother's leg when you were born.' But if you answered back, you only made things worse. Best just to get on with boning the trotters, or whatever. Once, he was telling us all some outlandish story about jumping off a train. Everyone was laughing. But then I said: 'Bullshit.' He picked up his knife, then he threw it down, then he grabbed me and put me up against the wall. It was almost like being back at home with Dad. Maybe that's how I was able to put up with it for so long.

Another classic occasion was when Stephen Terry, another of the chefs, attended his grandfather's funeral and made the mistake of going to the wake afterwards. When he got back a bit late, Marco said: 'I told you that you could go to the fucking funeral but that you couldn't go for tea and biscuits. I want you back in the fucking kitchen.' Steve was really crying. We were making tagliatelle that day, and Marco was shouting: 'Come on Steve, fucking turn it, fucking turn it, you cunt.' So he said: 'Yes, Marco, I'm fucking on my way.' That was it. Crash. Marco slapped him in the face.

'That's it,' he said. 'Get out of here. You may as well fuck off underground and join your granddad.'

After Jason Everett had left, we were all in the shit. Working at Harvey's was physically exhausting anyway. On Sundays, you would sleep all day. But once we were a man down, no one got any breaks at all. Then one day Marco called me upstairs to the office.

'I want you to do something for me,' he said. 'Jason is living in your flat, isn't he?'

'Yes.'

'Well, I've sacked him – and yet he's still in my kitchen.'

I had no idea what he meant.

'I mean that he's sleeping in your house, and you're working for me. When you come into work in the morning, you've slept under the same roof. I want you to go home tonight and kick him out. I want you to put his clothes, and all his knives, and any chef whites out on the street.'

I told Marco that I couldn't do this. I loved my job, but I couldn't do as he asked. 'Are you going to sack me?' I asked.

'Sit there,' he said. The next thing I knew, he was on the phone. He rings some restaurant, and says: 'Hi John, it's

Marco here. Look, I'm in the shit. My sous chef (that was me) is being fucking awkward.'

I couldn't believe it. Awkward? After all the work I'd done?

'So John, three cooks next Monday.' Then he put down the phone and said to me: 'You're leaving. You'll leave in a week's time. I want your notice.'

I went back downstairs. 'Everything okay?' said the guys. 'Yeah.'

I started making ravioli, because by then I was completely running the kitchen. I finished the first one and then something in me just snapped: I hurled it at the wall. Fuck this, I thought. I walked out and I went to the train station opposite, where I tore off my whites and threw them in the nearest bin. I went back to the flat in Clapham.

'What are you doing here?' asked Jason. 'It's only six o'clock.'

'Get changed, mate – we're going out to party. Marco's asked me to kick you out and I can't do that. He's told me I'm going in a week's time. Why should I wait a week?'

Fifteen minutes later, we're just getting changed when suddenly Steve Terry and another chef, Tim Hughes, and all the French waiters come in. 'Marco's closed the restaurant because you walked out,' says Steve. I couldn't believe it. The restaurant manager had to ring all the customers to make excuses for Marco closing the restaurant.

It was a Saturday night. We NEVER had a Saturday

night off. So we went to the Hammersmith Palais and we got absolutely mullered. The next night, we all piled off to a pub called the Sussex. All the chefs in London used to congregate at the Sussex on a Sunday. It was about nine o'clock. I was a bit tipsy when all of a sudden the music stopped and someone shouted: 'Is there a Gordon Ramsay in here?' There was a phone call for me behind the bar. When I took it, a voice said: 'Gordon. Marco.' I mouthed his name to all my mates and they all started shouting abuse.

'It's clear that you're with your mates,' he said. 'But I think we should talk.'

I told him that I had booked a holiday: I was off to Tenerife the next day.

'What are you going to that shit hole for?'

'Marco, after what you did to Jason and what you did to me, to be honest I can't take it any more. You've pushed me to my limit. I've got to go.'

But he was insistent; he needed to speak to me, and I gave in. Why? The truth is that, in spite of everything, he was a strong influence on me. I'd confided in him. The abuse I'd had from Dad had no point. But with Marco, the more he screwed you, the more he turned you over, the more you felt yourself becoming better. It sounds crazy, but I was becoming grateful for the bollockings. My saving grace was that I could take it physically, even when it was like SAS training camp.

We arranged that I would meet him at Harvey's at midnight.

I walked into the restaurant. It was pitch black. I thought: fantastic, he's not here. But when I switched on the lights, there he was, sitting in the corner of the room with a bottle of Badoit.

I started work again the next day.

How did he persuade me? 'Why are you throwing all this away?' he said. 'If you don't walk back into that kitchen tomorrow morning, you'll regret it for the rest of your life. I'll tell everyone that you ONCE worked here.' It felt like the moment I stepped out of the door, I would be shot.

And he was clever. He didn't back off. He made me feel special instead. He moved the goalposts. He pretty much gave me free run of Harvey's. When I did go back to work, I had an extra spring in my step. I was his right-hand man.

Essentially, though, the situation continued – the climate of fear. He never made mention of how good you were. New, talented cooks would come to work with us – older than me, more experienced than me – but they would never stay. They would tell me that I didn't need to take this shit, that it wasn't normal. It was okay to be ambitious and tenacious and fucking keen to cook, but I could have a life, too. The trouble was, it felt like those of us who lasted in his kitchen were Spitfires, and they were enemy planes, and every time one of them was shot down, all it meant to us was that there was another notch on our knife cases.

He could be totally irrational. I had difficulty understanding how his moods could fluctuate so much. It was only a few years later that I started to think: How can someone be so good, so dynamic one minute, and then three minutes later be completely different? It was only when I worked in other seriously good kitchens, and had something to compare Harvey's with, that I realised that despite his creative genius, Marco's behaviour was unnaturally erratic.

Breaks were out of the question, mostly. The only way you could get one was to take your shallots or your mushrooms and peel them while you were sitting out on the common, and woe betide you if he looked out of the office window and saw you kicking a ball around. You'd have to eat your Mars Bar and drink your Lucozade at the same time. We all looked like sad bulimics. One day, he was going out for lunch with Albert Roux. That meant we had to do lunch on our own, something that really excited me. However, he said that he was going to make the sauces for that evening's dinner when he came back from lunch. I thought to myself: oh, fuck, that means he's going to do the sauces just as we're going to slip out of the door for fifteen minutes. So I decided to do the sauces myself. I was so proud of them: the morel sauce, the red wine Hermitage sauce, the Madeira sauce, the fish velouté. About five minutes past twelve, just before he went out, he came to say goodbye. That's when he saw the sauces.

'What the fuck is going on here?' he said. 'Who finished

those sauces?' Steve Terry clammed up. Tim Hughes disappeared into his pastry. So I put my hand up.

'Marco, it was me. I finished them. I'm just about to bring them to the boil and cook them out for twenty minutes.'

The next thing you knew, it was like Baghdad. Pans were raining down on us. We hid behind the sorbet machine. He went mad. I mean, fucking mad. Finally, he threw the sauces themselves at us. Not only did that fuck up our fifteen-minute break; it put us in the shit for sauces that night. I was gutted. My eyes filled up. There was nothing bloody wrong with those sauces. He didn't even taste them.

Another time, there was an incident involving a leek terrine. It was a very famous leek terrine. It was filled with langoustine or lobster or Dublin Bay prawns, but we used to keep one end free of the langoustines for vegetarians, which we marked with a piece of blue tape. It was a terrine that was pressed for two and a half hours, a hundred quid a throw. Perhaps this was why, even though we were all perfectly competent, we weren't allowed to slice it. Only Marco was allowed to slice it. Anyway, during one service, he barked at me: 'Right, vegetarian. Which end is the vegetarian end?' I told him the end with the tape but by then he'd already turned the bloody thing round. That effectively meant that he was slicing the wrong end. So I pointed out his mistake.

'You fucking forgot,' he said. 'You don't know which

end is which.' Yet still, he carried on slicing, and each time he cut a slice, he would throw it at me. On and on he went, slicing and throwing, until he was halfway through the terrine. 'Don't you dare speak to me,' he said.

'But Marco, you've got the wrong end.'

He picked up what was left of the terrine and threw it at me. I looked like Worzel Gummidge only where there should have been straw, I had leeks. The maître d' was told to tell the customer that there was a problem with the terrine, and Marco wasn't happy with it. That was another time that I walked out, only he ran down the road after me, and called me back. He didn't apologise, though.

I stayed at Harvey's for two years and ten months. It was a massive learning curve for me, and it completely changed the way that I cooked.

The trouble was that Marco made you feel as though there was nothing outside of Harvey's, that nowhere else mattered. That was just not true. Even if I hadn't been sick to the bottom of my stomach of the rages and the bullying and violence, I needed to spread my wings if I was ever going to become the kind of cook I now so desperately wanted to be. And that is exactly what I did next.

CHAPTER FOUR
FRENCH LEAVE

I LANDED A job with Alain Ducasse in Paris but, of course, Marco wasn't having any of it. 'You're fucking stupid,' he said. 'You won't last. Get yourself into a French kitchen in THIS country before you go off to France. I'll get you into Le Gavroche.'

Le Gavroche has been open since the 1960s. It's now run by my friend Michel Roux Junior, a fellow marathon runner, but in those days the man in the kitchen was still Albert, his father. I didn't really want to work for Albert. Marco had worked for every top classical chef in the country – Nico Ladenis, Raymond Blanc, Albert Roux, Pierre Koffmann – and now he could cook just as well as them. In turn, I'd taken everything I possibly could from him, so what would be the point of me going back to his teachers? On the other hand, it was, and still is, a place where the spirit of Escoffier is alive and kicking, so it was EXACTLY the kind of establishment I wanted to work in, even if it was in Mayfair rather than Montparnasse. And there was another attraction. The really great thing about it, from my point of view, was that it was only open Monday to Friday; for the first time in my life, I'd be able to enjoy a proper weekend. Well, that was the theory.

I was in the shit, financially. Things were bad in the flat in Clapham that my colleague Steve Terry and I owned. Our mortgage was £1,600 a month and it was a nightmare. We'd only borrowed £70,000 in the first place, but in 1988, interest rates were just going mad. We were so fucking screwed for money.

When I got to Le Gavroche, I said: 'I'm really pleased to be here; thank you so much for allowing me to come here; yes, sir, no, sir, three bags full, sir.' Then I went straight back to being a commis chef. In other words, I was on less money anyway, and as a result, more in the shit than ever. So Saturday nights, I would go back to Harvey's and work there, so that Marco could take the night off. I was still the only person he trusted to run that place – except doing that was a bit harder now. The staff was in mutiny, turning their back on me whenever I walked in. You couldn't blame them, I suppose. They never saw me Monday to Friday, then all of a sudden I'm there bossing them around again. For this pleasure, I was paid £50 a throw.

It was unbelievably tough. At Le Gavroche, you had to be there at 6.30 a.m. You needed every bit of energy and if you lagged behind, you were out on your ear, looking for a new job. A rumour went round that I was moonlighting at Harvey's. I was very nervous. One Saturday night, Albert and Michel, his brother, were coming into Harvey's for dinner. I was terrified, in case they saw me in the kitchen. I was shitting myself. I said to Marco: 'Look, I'm absolutely fucked. I'm spending all day in bed on Sunday, and, come 5.30 a.m. on Monday morning, I just can't get out of bed. I'm too knackered.' I know of at least one chef who used to sleep in the kitchen at Le Gavroche, Sunday nights, so he was ready for the next morning. That's how the regime affected you if you weren't on top of things.

Michel, Albert's son, had pretty much detected that I was working at Harvey's. So I told him the truth. He went mad, I mean really mad. But he's an amazing guy – he lent me some money so that I didn't have to go to Harvey's any more. 'Look,' he said. 'Just pay me back later.' Until then, Marco had been ringing Le Gavroche every five minutes, trying to find out how I was doing, putting pressure on me. At last, I could concentrate again.

Of course, I've had my differences with the Roux family. Albert was a great chef, and Michel Jnr is now a mate. He was great to work with: after a good service, you got a beer and a pat on the back. But Michel Snr, well, let's just say that he and I are not each other's greatest fans. A few years ago, he slagged off *Kitchen Nightmares*, my Channel 4 TV show, and had a go at me personally, insisting that you can't hang on to three Michelin stars unless you are in the kitchen all the time. Well, I was fucking proud of that show and it went on to win a BAFTA. I have never got on with him and although I admire his cooking, I've never really warmed to him as a person.

Albert asked me if I would go and work with him at a place called Hotel Diva, a ski resort in the French Alps in a place called Isola, just above Nice, where he was a consultant. The idea was that I would be his number two. I went for one season and it was amazing, a kind of working holiday. Somewhere to start learning French, and to start understanding France. I briefly got myself a French girl-friend (though I still had a girlfriend back at home – which meant that I had quite a lot of explaining to do when she wondered out loud how I'd become so fluent, so quickly). I was only twenty-three, but I think that Albert had started to see how genuinely obsessed I was with the idea of France. And for me, it seemed like a miracle. At Stratford High, lots of the kids would go off on skiing trips – but never us, of course, because we couldn't afford it. Finally, I was skiing! I made a complete prat of myself the first time I skied, of course – I insisted on just going straight down the slope, no lessons, always learning the hard way.

The kitchen out there was a challenge as my French was so poor, I couldn't tell anyone what to do. I'd met Jean-Claude, who's now my maître d' at *Royal Hospital Road*, at Le Gavroche, and he came out to Diva with us, and he'd have to translate what customers said. But it was a great experience. The head chef at Diva, Alan McLellan, was an American guy whose nickname was 'Cowboy'. He was a sweet guy but he had a palate like a cow's backside and on one occasion a couple who'd been in when he was running the kitchen had complained. The following night I was in charge in Alan's absence and the same couple had come back to eat. As they finished dinner Jean-Claude came through into the kitchen going: 'Ooh la la, the guests on table seven say their dinner was absolutely amazing.' I could hardly believe my ears.

There was a cookery school there as well, and we'd get all these big coaches full of people who'd bought holidays via newspaper promotions turning up. They'd ski during the day, take cookery lessons at night, and then enjoy a great big gourmet dinner. Albert would turn up for three days at a time, and everything had to be right, from the croissants to the room service.

One night, we had to put on an eight-course tasting menu for a massive group of *Mail on Sunday* readers. I was running the fish and the meat, and my head chef, Alan, was running the bouillabaisse, which was the starter. He'd made it that morning but rather than putting it in the fridge to cool down, he put it in these stainless steel buckets and then sent the young apprentices outside with them to put them in the snow. The trouble was that it was minus ten degrees out there, so the stuff was freezing over on the surface as it was cooling down, while beneath it was still warm. This made it fester, like a bowl of yeast. And Alan completely forgot to bring them in, and skim them to take the fat off.

Champagne and canapés were served and then everyone sat down for dinner. 'Fucking hell,' he said. 'Get me the bouillabaisse, Ramsay.' That was when he remembered that it was still outside. Out I went. By this time, the buckets were beneath a huge great snow drift. I scraped the ice off, pushed my fingers into a bucket, and it was horrible, like fucking hot Parmesan cheese. Disgusting.

I came running in with the buckets.

'Give it to me, they're fucking sitting down,' he yelled.

'You'd better take a look, first,' I said.

Then in walks Albert, screaming that he wants to taste a cup of the bouillabaisse. At this point, Alan, the head chef, decides that he wants me to take the blame for the cock-up.

'No fucking way,' I said. 'I will not lie to Albert Roux.'

Lying is the biggest sin you can commit in a kitchen. Working with someone who lies to you is worse than working with someone who can't cook. Rather than admit his mistake, he brought it to the boil, skimmed off the froth and the natural yeast, and tipped in a bit of brandy. Then he gave it to Albert. Well, fuck me. I felt like an avalanche was coming down on top of the Hotel Diva. He went ballistic. Absolutely ballistic. He got hold of the bucket and he just threw it. He was aiming for Alan, but it was the kitchen

My mum, Helen, second right, before she was married, with some of the other girls from the nurses' home. It's heartbreaking how young and pretty and full of hope she looks.

Me, aged about four, in Glasgow. Sweet, eh?

ABOVE: Me and Diane, my older sister.
We're pretending to play a couple of dad's guitars.

BELOW: This is a school photograph. I'm on the left, aged about seven, in the middle is Yvonne, my younger sister, on the right is Ronnie.

One of Dad's promotional shots in the Banbury days.

BOYS' UNDER 14s
Sackville Rovers 6,
Badsey Colts 5

IT needed extra time before this very exciting and close game was settled.

Sackville took the lead after 30 seconds with a goal from Keaney. Davies levelled but Badsey with the first of his three goals.

The play was very even with both goalkeepers given plenty to do. Ramsey scored for Sackville, only to see Badsey level again when Davies scored from a penalty. He soon completed his scoring for the afternoon giving Badsey the lead. Hensher scored for Sackville on the stroke of half time, to make the score at the interval 3-3.

Badsey broke through for Tropman to score for the visitors to take the lead again. They held on to their lead till near the end of normal time when Ramsey scored for Sackville to take the game into extra time.

The home team scored with a goal from Compton only for Badsey to equalise through Tropman.

When a replay seemed certain Sackville scored the winner when Bath scored from a cross from Ramsey.

Both teams deserved the highest compliments on a very good game played under tricky conditions.

Stratford Alliance U14
Sackville Rovers 6 Mill Utd 1

IN a very even and exciting first half both sides scored through defensive errors. Sackville were the first to score when Gordon Ramsey beat the Mill keeper to a poor back pass after 15 minutes. Ten minutes later Mill were level when Ben Richardson took advantage of a defensive mix-up to shoot home.

Ten minutes into the second half Mark Hensher ran onto a through ball from Ramsey to put Sackville in front. From then on it was all Sackville. Their third came when Ramsey pushed home a Jardine cross. Hensher got the fourth after good midfield work by Bath.

Ramsey completed a hat-trick, his second in consecutive games and Mark Trinder rounded things off for Sackville after some persistent play.

Sackville Rovers 6 Alveston 3

ALVESTON put Sackville's defence under a lot of pressure in the first ten minutes, but failed to make the most of some fine attacks with Gillett, the Sackville keeper, being able to cope well.

Sackville scored with their first real attack when Ramsey ran on to a through ball from the midfield to beat Bedwin with a well placed shot.

The play was very even with both sides going close to adding to the score. It fell to Ramsey to score the second of his four goals after twenty minutes.

Alveston soon got into their stride after the interval, and Jeremy Graham scored with a well – taken goal, shooting through a ruck of players. Within a minute Alister Graham put the teams level with a long shot.

Sackville picked themselves up after these setbacks and were soon back in front with Ramsey completing his scoring with two well-taken goals to give his side a 4-2 lead. Harper made it five for the home team.

The visitors were still playing well and got their third goal when they were awarded a penalty. Jeremy Graham converted.

Harper ended the scoring for the afternoon when he ran onto a very good chip from Trinder to beat the visitors' keeper with a low shot.

Alveston 3
Sackville Rovers 5

HUNT gave Alveston an early lead but Sackville's Bath equalised a few minutes later.

Bath scored a second goal to give Sackville a 2-1 lead approaching half time but Wallington managed to pull back the deficit just before the break. Half time 2-2.

Ramsey gave Sackville the lead yet again but Alveston took advantage of a poor clearance and Bayliss scored to make it 3-3.

Ramsey scored again with the goal of the match when he beat three players on the edge of the area before shooting high into the net.

And Bath completed his hat-trick to give Sackville a 5-3 win.

South Warwickshire Schools Football Association
Oxford United Cup
South Warwickshire Schools U13s 1, Swindon Schools U13s 4

SOUTH Warwickshire Under 13s failed to qualify for the finals of this competition losing to Swindon boys in a fine display of schools' soccer.

On a sticky Studley pitch the home side opened strongly and pressed for most of the first 15 minutes and indeed after constant pressure a Swindon defender headed against his own bar from a cross by Macer Nash, following fine work by Gordon Ramsey.

Somewhat against the run of play the visitors took the lead when the central striker scored with a speculative shot from 25 yards.

The second half saw Swindon steadily take over the dominant role with some aggressive ball winning and some fine close passing movements and soon they added an excellent second goal.

Meanwhile, the hero of the hour was turning out to be their goalkeeper, John Barnes, who having made three excellent first half saves added to them with a string of fine handling and blocking saves. He nearly made a brilliant two-handed save for Swindon's third goal but the ball unluckily dropped under the bar. Further pressure and an early cross caused havoc in the home defence and the ball was turned in at the far post.

The scoreline somewhat flattered Swindon and a goal was no more than South Warwickshire deserved. Five minutes from time Nash was

but
to
man
who
make the
Metropo

the arrears.

Team: J Barnes (Greville), H Mackinnon (Henley), G Mason (Alcester), A Haines (Stratford), N Niblet (Stratford), M Walke (Henley), A Hill (Studley), Bath (Stratford), I Wilso (Greville), M Nash (Bidford), Ramsey (Stratford), S Syk (Henley).

LEFT: Some of my early column inches.

RIGHT: Showing off our silverware. I'm third in from the left.

LEFT: South Warwickshire Schools Cup U13s. I'm in the back row, third from the left.

RIGHT: Team picture of Sackville Rovers at the Stratford Town ground. I'm at the back, far right.

Team picture of Sackville Rovers at the Stratford Town ground who beat Badsey Juniors 10-1 last Sunday in a Stratford Alliance Boys' U14 match. Back row (from left) Paul Charman, Steve Morris, Craig Edkins, Adrian Gillett, Andrew Maines, Kevin Bath, Gordon Ramsey. Front row (from left) Nigel Harper, Darren Gran...... w Barrowman, Mark Hensher, Garry Compton and ...... ascot Philip Andrews.

Me, aged 11, in my Stratford Town Juniors kit. On the left is Kevin Bath, aka 'Bathy'; on the right is Mark Hensher.

Me, Dad and Ronnie in Torquay, 1979. Dad was 36, I would have been 12 and Ronnie 11.

Fishing in Brixham, Devon, with Dad, aged about 12. I'm holding a gar fish, a species that tends to swim in front of mackerel. It's about the same size as my widger ...

ABOVE: This is a photo from my Rangers days – a combination of first team players and youth team players assembled for a testimonial match against East Kilbride. I'm in the second row, far left. On the far right of the same row is Ally McCoist, who'd just made it into the first team. In the front row, far left, is Derek Ferguson, future captain of Scotland. Ian Ferguson is in the back row, far left, and Dave McPherson is in the back row, in the middle.

BELOW: Me, aged 16, photographed with Broughton and North Newington FC, my Saturday side in Banbury. Look at all those mullets!

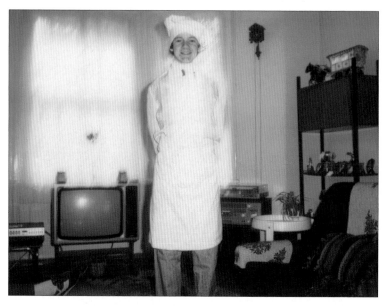

ABOVE: Me in my first set of chef's whites, bought by the Banbury Round Table. I was so proud of those whites. Now, of course, I think that I look like a complete twat. I wouldn't be seen dead in that hat now.

BELOW: Me in the British Virgin Islands, in the days when I was working for Reg Grundy on his private yacht. I am in desperate need of a hair cut.

porter who took most of it. There was saffron and tomatoes everywhere, bubbling across every wall like some kind of alien ectoplasm. The place was caked in it. What happened next? Albert went out there, and made a speech. And while he made that speech, we made bouillabaisse to order, from scratch. It took us forty-five minutes. I've never seen a serious soup made so quickly. I spread it between six pans, and there were fourteen of us dashing between them, crushing it, and blitzing it, and skimming it – eighty portions in all. What a nightmare.

It was a dreamy kind of time, those fifteen weeks. There was a little twenty-seat cinema there. All the films were in French. I used to go and watch them, listening to the French dumbly, hoping to absorb by osmosis anything I could – and then I'd go home to bed and put my Linguaphone tapes on. Same deal. I'd lie there, looking at these amazing mountains, and at the chairlifts dripping with icicles. In the morning, you'd wake up to the loud bangs as they set off little deliberate avalanches to clear the piste. The air was fresh, and my head was clear, and within two months, I was getting the accent and the pronunciation right. After that, I refused to speak any English. I still can't write French for toffee – unless I'm putting down a menu. And I can tell someone what to do in a kitchen, and that's all that really matters.

*   *   *

From the ski slopes, I made my way – at last – to Paris. There, I went down to an even lower salary – the French government's minimum wage. It was the bottom of the bottom. Miles worse even than being an apprentice. But believe me, as a Brit in a French kitchen, they weren't going to pay me proper money. It worked out at about £480 a month.

Luckily, I was subsidised by my then girlfriend. Albert's PA was a girl called Rosalind, and she'd been my girlfriend at Le Gavroche. We met at a Christmas party so, of course, everybody said that we were shagging because I wanted to make sure I got a good reference. She was nine years older than me, you see. But it wasn't that. Anyway, she'd lived in Paris before, and she was determined to follow me out there. She got a fantastic job, and we got a flat, and she picked up most of the bills. I'll never forget that – the help she gave me when I needed it most. There's no two ways about it; she was amazing – though we don't talk now, it all ended rather badly.

Paris was wonderful: scurrying round the markets, working in cafés learning how to make lattes and cappuccinos, or turning out a decent salad. Just discovering how to do the simplest things, correctly. But I was so hard up. After I'd paid my share of the rent, I had about eighty quid left a month. It was humiliating in a way, like being back at school and getting my free dinners. Under French law, my employer was required to give me back half of my Métro fare. So every Monday, I had to go up with my little orange tickets to get back my ten francs. Still, I had a massive sense of purpose: this was where I was meant to be.

My first job was at Guy Savoy, which had two Michelin stars and when I first walked into that kitchen, I'd never felt so remote, so far removed from anywhere in my entire life. Everyone was ignoring me. Even the kitchen porters had no respect for me. On my first day, somebody nicked my socks.

No one was interested that I'd come from a three-star restaurant. All they knew was that I was a 'rosbif' and, as such, I should learn my place. For the first three months, I was in pastry, turning sorbet machines. The most exciting thing about turning a sorbet is, well, there's nothing exciting at all about turning a sorbet machine – unless you count the fact that you start it the minute the customer places their order so that the ice is light and aerated. There were ten machines, turning ten different flavours. I'd put together these exotic fruit salads and these amazing chocolate sorbets and then they'd been taken to the table on a trolley. I could scoop quenelles out with one hand. Beautiful. The trouble was, I knew how to cook, and they had no idea! I'd worked in two of the best restaurants in Britain. I'd spent all this time in the south of France. But they didn't give a fuck. They weren't interested in the slightest. Not until my French was more fluent. And even once it was, I had to wait my turn. The pastry chef was a little squirt. I had to sharpen his knives every day, and I had to sweep up while he was working. He'd shout at me: sweep the floor. It was obvious how much pleasure he got out of watching me sweeping between his legs. I had to fetch his lunch and his dinner and his espressos. Luckily, I'd taken an extra job in a café, so every time I put a cup of coffee in front of his smug little face, at least I knew he was never going to argue with it. It was the most amazing coffee he would ever drink. If he was trying to break me – well, the bigger an arsehole he was, the more it helped me keep going.

My time as king of the sorbets was a real test of my patience. I could have gone back to London, taken a nice job with some decent money. But a little voice was telling me to keep going – that the longer I trained, the more that would eventually come my way. In Paris, I learned total respect for food, and how cleverly you can make something out of nothing. Take a leek. At Harvey's, we would take a forty-inch leek and use about half of it – half an inch of white stuff to finish a soup or to use as a garnish. The rest of it would be binned. In France, you'd use the best white bit for the soup, but then you'd use the rest for a sauce, the top of it for a mousse, and then the very top of it, you'd use in a staff meal. Nothing went in the bin. The way that they roasted the most amazing capons and guinea fowl. The way they cooked calf's liver. And the way that every afternoon, every little arrondissement had its own market. The chef would order in such small quantities: sixteen tomatoes, or a dozen shallots, or just two sea bass. It was all about precision, and freshness. My eyes were opened.

The pastry section was downstairs. Of course, I was dying to get upstairs, and I was always eavesdropping from the bottom of the stairs, listening to what was going on. I hated every minute of making pastry, but you could say that I'm glad of it now.

We used to make beautiful caramelised apple tarts served with a black pepper custard. We would produce the most amazing pink grapefruit terrine pressed with a coriander jelly and served with an Earl Grey sorbet. Then there was the crème brûlée with roasted rhubarb served with a fresh Granny Smith apple that had been frozen and juiced. It came in a shot glass, this wonderful green film to be poured over the brûlée itself. It makes me sigh just thinking about them all, even now. They were just fucking fantastic.

It took me three months to get upstairs. They put me on fish, one of the most difficult stations of all. A baptism of fire. Fish demands precision. There's no such thing as 'medium' or 'rare' when it comes to fish. Thirty seconds too much cooking can mean that the bass is dry, ruined. But the minute I was there, I was away, there was no stopping me: I swear that I had the biggest penis in all of France.

The first thing that I cooked was a sea bass. The sauce was made from an amazing fish stock infused with vanilla.

You whisked it up with lots of butter, so that it was almost a mousse. The thing I could never understand, though, was that for the first and only time in my entire cooking life, when we came to roast the bass, they left the scales on. When you sautéed the fish, they sort of spiked up, so it started to look like a hedgehog. Chef said that some of the most sought-after flavour was in the scales, but all I knew was that every single plate came back with the scales still on it. So while it looked amazing, it obviously tasted like shit. 'Chef,' I said. 'I can scale it for you.' But he went bananas, as if I was trying to tell him what to do. I've still got the utmost respect for Guy Savoy – he is the most amazing chef I've ever worked with – but to this day, he serves bass with the scales on. Bizarre. Others of his dishes, though, were touched with genius, as if the bottom of the sea had met the earth, if that doesn't sound too poncey for words. I remember a wonderful crab risotto finished with a sea urchin butter.

When you're on fish, you're next to the meat and you're opposite the veg, and timing is everything, so you're always watching what everyone else is up to. I was such a proud cock. I was always the first man to get into the kitchen, and my eyes were always on stalks. Perhaps that's why Guy took a shine to me, because we were soon getting on like a house on fire. Within two weeks of being upstairs, he'd given me tickets for an England football match. I won his respect. I don't care what anyone says, you have to work twice as hard as anyone else if you're an Englishman in a French kitchen. I was first in and last out, and I used to beg him to let me make the staff dinner. The only way I could survive there was to cook my arse off, making sure that I didn't fall down, break down or cave in. I stood fucking strong. After a month on fish, I was as strong as an ox and my French was improving. I'd been in Paris for four months, and things were moving at a thousand miles an hour. I was promoted to a senior chef position, and I felt so special. But still, I kept going. I wouldn't take my half-day off during the week. We were required to take it by law, but I just wouldn't go. I would come in and work for nothing. I couldn't do the fish because, since it was supposed to be my day off, my number two would be working that, so I'd volunteer to go on the veg instead. Of course, my colleagues didn't like this. The little British brown-nose! So they'd start blanking me, or speaking so fast I would struggle to follow them. And someone carried on nicking my socks. A pair would disappear every time I used to get changed – something that never used to happen to any of the other chefs. Soon, though, Guy was coming up to me in the middle of service and pinching me, or telling me jokes. They were in French, so I didn't really have a clue, but I would wait till he delivered what was obviously his punchline, and then laugh along with him, and then get back to the food. English customers would come, and he would be adamant that they be taken into the kitchen to meet me, his little British chef, because he knew how homesick, how lonely, how isolated I was. He saw through my arrogance, my pushiness; he knew how hard I worked. I was like an orphan there, and he stepped in as a father-figure. People sometimes point out how, in shows like *Kitchen Nightmares*, I'll always encourage the youngest chap in the kitchen, the porter or the pot washer, the little snot that no one else notices or cares about. If you want to know why – Paris is why. I know how it feels to be in a corner, unnoticed and unloved.

Then I heard that, back home, Albert had put me up for the National Chef of the Year competition, and that I'd reached the semi-final. I begged chef for a day off.

'What is this bullshit?' he said. 'You're not a chef.'

'Yeah, but I'm training to be a chef, and I really want to win this.'

So I chose a few of Guy's dishes, went off to London and won my semi-final. He was over the moon that I'd cooked his dishes and was now certain that I was going to win the whole thing. All the other competitors in the final had much grander positions than me. They were all 'executive' this and 'executive' that, but under my name it just said: Gordon Ramsay, commis. All the other entrants could see was the lowly word 'commis'; the fact that I was working for Guy Savoy meant fuck-all to them. Still, they were soon laughing on the other side of their faces because I took three days off and I won the fucker. I made an amazing risotto, a ravioli of lobster, and that famous crème brûlée with a jus Granny Smith, and in return I won £2,000, which helped to pay me through Paris for a bit longer, and an amazing Wedgwood cigar box. I said to the organisers, thanks very much for that but I don't smoke. So they re-lined it for me, and it became a jewellery box, and Mum still keeps her bits and pieces in it to this very day.

I got back to Paris, and I showed chef the menu and the photographs and the cheque, and he was so pleased – he alone out of the whole brigade.

It was a while later, after I'd been in his kitchen for a year, that I told him I wanted to move on, to try another kitchen. That was when he offered me a job as his number two. I was thrilled, but I didn't take it. I knew that as a number two, I wouldn't learn anything; I would have to show other people what to do. And I didn't want that, I wasn't ready to cap my training so soon. For another thing, I'd already been a number two – to Marco, and at Le Gavroche. I wasn't going to do that job for a third time. So I went to the great Joël Robuchon where – guess what? – I had to start from the beginning all over again. Yes, believe it or not, I went straight back to being a humble commis. Again. And this time the humiliation was on a whole new level.

Robuchon was the most famous restaurant in the world at the time. It had just forty-five seats, and was as snooty as they come – and I'm talking about the way they treated us, not the customers. When you arrived at the restaurant, you had to ring a bell and then stand there while one of the waiting staff let you in. You had a key, but you weren't allowed to use it. Robuchon himself had a lavatory that only he and his wife were allowed to use. The kitchen was in a kind of corridor. Once you were installed there, you simply didn't move for the next five hours, and it was like the fucking SAS. Robuchon made Marco look like a fucking pussy cat. It was extraordinary.

He was the first chef who was at all like Marco in terms of temperament when in the kitchen, but because he was older and so much more celebrated and accomplished than Marco, I couldn't understand WHY. When I joined him, he was forty-nine. Two weeks later, he announced that he was going to retire within a year, and within twenty-four hours, the restaurant was fully booked for a year (these days, of course, he is back out of retirement and, like me, is running a world-wide restaurant empire, with joints in Las Vegas and Japan). This news made me doubly lucky to have a place there. The doors were locked, but I'd got my job. I lasted for ten months.

It was much more difficult to move up through the ranks at Robuchon. Impossible, in fact. The hierarchy was incredible. Every section had its own sous chef, and then there was Robuchon's right hand man, Bernard Michel – he's still there now because he bought the place off

Robuchon, though he's only got two stars now, whereas Robuchon had three. Every year, without fail, I send him congratulations for maintaining his two stars. Every fucking year. 'Best wishes,' I write, 'on keeping your two stars.' Then I imagine him going green like the Incredible Hulk with envy because I've got three.

It was interesting working at Robuchon because the cooking was very classical, but they also served things like a fillet of hake, breaded and deep fried and served with half a lemon, which was more like something you'd expect to find in, say, The Ivy. Or a prawn salad with mayonnaise and these little dots of ketchup arranged around the edge of the plate. I could never understand that dish. But then next to it, you'd have this amazing roast sea bass with a caramelised tomato ketchup sauce. It tasted fantastic – not that I had much chance to eat anything. We didn't have time to eat. We were right back to a Harvey's-type situation again, where there's so much to do, where you're so far in the shit, that you can't stop, not even for a minute. The floor was always wet, and the kitchen porters were the kingpins. Robuchon's hot plate was at eye level, so you'd walk up to it, and put your food on it, and his eyes would be all over the place. Normally, with a hot plate, the chef looks down on the food. But not there. It was oddly terrifying. It made you feel scrutinised, naked, like you had nowhere to hide.

Lo and behold, I was on the fish, wrestling with the

langoustines. Talk about déjà vu. I'd been there for three months when this guy walks in. He winked at me, and I winked back at him. Fuck me if it wasn't Michael Caines, now at Gidleigh Park in Devon, where he has two Michelin stars in spite of the fact that, in 1994, he lost an arm in a car accident. He'd just come from working for Bernard Loiseau in Saulieu, a chef whose name is well-known in this country now because in 2003 he committed suicide, an act some people have connected to the fact that he had recently lost two points in Gault Millau Guide. So there we were, the two 'rosbifs', him on meat, me on fish, surrounded by all these Frogs. It was the toughest kitchen in the world, but we were glad to be there. You wanted to get a year of it under your belt. I learned a lot, but perhaps not as much as I did with Guy Savoy. Savoy was hungry, he was pushing for three stars. Robuchon was fantastic at the classical stuff, but there wasn't much flair. He wasn't into change; he was into heritage.

The French chefs often gave me a hard time for being slow, but I would rather be slow and get it right. But they were always on my bollocks, anyway. About three months in, there was a terrible scene involving a plate of ravioli. The ravioli in question were more like dim sum – made without any egg yolk. They were filled with Dublin Bay prawns rolled in a truffle, five of them on the plate, some cabbage in the middle, and a really light foie gras sauce. The ravioli order came in and, for the first time in my life, blow me if people hadn't ordered it 'medium', 'medium rare' and 'well done'. They didn't want them to be too translucent, I suppose. This completely freaked me out. One table had ordered three portions of the ravioli, each one cooked a different way.

'Allez, allez,' said Bernard. 'Cook, cook.' Then the fucker put all fifteen raviolis in the water at the same time. Really, the three portions should have each gone in two minutes apart.

'Look,' I said. 'There are three different . . .' But he was on my case before I could even finish my sentence.

'ALLEZ! Do as you're fucking told.'

I had to take them out one at a time. I knew it wasn't going to work.

I took them to the hot plate, and it was too hot. That split the sauce, and it bubbled and congealed. Robuchon could see what was happening. He touched one of the ravioli, and said: 'Which one is that?'

'The first one is rare,' I said. Of course, it wasn't. Everything was the wrong way round. If that wasn't the rare one, where the fuck WAS the rare one? Wherever it was, it wasn't going to be rare by the time he got hold of it.

Robuchon got hold of the plate, and threw it at me. It hit the side of my face. My ear was blocked with hot food, my face was burnt, and there was ravioli all over the place. I apologised, and started all over again.

I couldn't go to Bernard and start on the recriminations

with him because his job was screwing you on your section, punishing you until you cracked and you couldn't come in the next day. He had a reputation for going through between four and six chefs a week. But what he didn't seem to realise was that I'd come from Guy Savoy. I didn't send in my CV and knock on the fucking door. Guy had put in a call to Robuchon. Of course, Robuchon wasn't going to turn round and say, look, he's from Guy Savoy, look after him. Robuchon was on my back from day one, but he didn't totally BRAIN me – that's the most important thing. There is a difference, believe it or not.

In fact, that bollocking was nothing. One evening, we had eight Japanese investors in: duck for two, two ordered a meat course, and four fish. I'll never forget it. The duck was cooked en croûte. So that would come out of the oven, and then you had two minutes before the other main courses all had to be ready. Timing was crucial. One of the fish I had to cook was the hake. I had to wait until all the breadcrumbs were the same colour, then I had to take it out and pipe on this butter – God, it was the most ghastly dish I've ever seen in a three-star establishment – and I was also doing John Dory and sea bass, two minutes, timing myself by this clock on the hearth. You're down to thirty seconds to go and, trust me, when the shit hits the fan, no one helps you: you're on your fucking jack. All of a sudden, Bernard has fucked up. There was a problem with the pastry, and he was in such a rage about it that he slammed the oven door, and the glass broke, the donkey. It all kicked off from there. A minute later, I heard screaming, and then I saw this huge copper pan coming at us – the pan that the duck was supposed to be in. It turned out that what had happened was the meat section had panicked and forgotten to put the duck IN. Someone had lifted the lid up and discovered this and, well, I've never heard a scream like it. I can still hear it today. It was mayhem. The guy had to start again from scratch. It was a horrific night, and I swear to God that if there had been a back door, I think we would all have bolted.

I was twenty-five, but I was taking shit like a fifteen-year-old. Michael and I would wait for the dessert trolley to come back out of the dining room, then we'd take whatever we could to eat. Michael was good – he'd always get me a chocolate tart, or an amazing crumble. We were starving. I was like a fucking rake. The restaurant was closed at the weekend, but you had to be in every weekday by six, and you wouldn't get home before one. Friday nights, we'd go to a lovely big old brasserie at the Trocadero and sit looking at the lights of the Eiffel Tower until four o'clock in the morning, talking about who'd been fucked the most that week, and who was on their way out. We were like ghosts. There'd be eight of us – some German who looked like he was about to die, some American standing there, gaunt and white like an addict, three or four French, and us two. At the end of the night, we'd each put a hand palm up on the table with our key to the kitchen in it, according to whether or not we'd be in the kitchen next week. Normally, at least three people's hands would be empty. They'd already left their keys behind at the office – because Bernard was obsessed with getting his keys back. That was all he was interested in – he certainly didn't care where you were off to.

Robuchon was such an unpleasant person to work for. To the French public, he portrayed himself as cool and sophisticated, the real deal. But in the kitchen, he was just a tyrant. If he threw a plate at you, you weren't to expect an apology. The next day, he wouldn't even say 'good morning' to you. Once you knew you were leaving, your sole ambition became a desire to pee in his private toilet. I bet every single departing chef made a point of doing that. I know I did. At the end of my stint, they stopped my last month's salary, who knows why? I think it was to try and make me stay a bit longer. On my last week, the fucker even put me on bin duty. You literally had to climb inside the bins on a Saturday morning and hose them down for about three hours. A terrible job.

'But it's my last day, tomorrow,' I said to chef.

'Look, you'll be here tomorrow morning, cleaning those bins out, or you'll never work in a Michelin star restaurant again. I'll ring every chef in France and make sure that you're banned.'

That night, I knew I wouldn't get my money. I knew in

my bones that I had worked the entire last month for nothing.

Perhaps you're wondering what my relationship with Robuchon is like now. After all, today, we're rivals on the international stage; the pair of us own and run some of the finest restaurants in the world. Well, it's weird, and very 'celebrity love-in'. Our paths cross often. Robuchon was interested in opening a restaurant at the Grosvenor Square Marriott (he didn't get it; that's where we now have the acclaimed *maze*; the chef is Jason Atherton, who used to cook at our Dubai restaurant, *Verre*) and he came to *Claridge's* with his partner for a meeting one day when I was overseeing service and we bumped into one another. All of a sudden, he's embracing me. 'It's so good to see you,' he said. 'I'm so glad that you're doing well.' I could hardly believe my ears. The fucker doesn't know me from Adam. He didn't get close to his cooks – we were just skivvies. It was almost funny, in a way. I thought: You don't mean a word you're saying. I mean, he was kissing and hugging me like I'm his long-lost son.

After my stint at Robuchon, I knew I was good for nothing – at least not for a while. Physically, I was broken. I had nothing left to give. I needed time out. But that was easier said than done. I couldn't afford not to work. I was beyond broke. What I needed was a lucky break – a way of earning some cash and rebooting at the same time. That break came to me when a man called Pierre, a boat chartering agent, appeared just in the nick of time. He saved my life as it were and before long, I was off on another adventure – and this time, believe it or not, the money was good, and the hours were human.

CHAPTER FIVE
OCEANS APART

A GUY CAME into the restaurant who had some kind of agency near Nice that specialised in employing chefs to work on board the yachts of millionaires. He made it clear that these guys earned a lot of money. He wasn't exactly offering me a job straight off, but he was making it clear that they were in desperate need of reputable chefs; most of those they attracted into this kind of work were the kind of men who were running away from something. So a few days later, I sent them my CV, and within twenty-four hours they contacted me and told me that they had a job for me on board a charter. The captain was reputed to like a drink, but lots of tips were promised. The idea of what amounted to a working holiday – sun, sea, sand – sounded like just what the doctor ordered.

So I headed down to the Med. My boat, if my memory is right, was called *Blue Crystal*, and it was captained by an absolute knob. But berthed next to it was another boat,

Idlewood. One night, I got talking to one of its deck hands, and he let me know that they were looking for a chef, too – theirs had had some kind of family crisis and disappeared.

'Our captain's called Ginger Steve,' he said.

Christ, I thought.

I met up with Ginger Steve two days later, and gave him all my papers. He asked me if I was absolutely sure that this was what I wanted to do – work on *Idlewood*. 'Yeah, yeah, honestly,' I said. 'I've never worked on a boat before, but I want to try and save some money so I can start my own restaurant in London.' He told me that he worked for a high-profile couple, but that he couldn't tell me who they were; in other words, this was not some charter boat, this was a private yacht, which meant that its owners, whoever they were, had to be seriously rich. I told the captain on the *Blue Crystal* that I was off.

Needless to say, he wasn't best pleased. He had a lot of charters booked. We started fighting, and he tried to slap me – at which point, I literally boat-hopped. The following day, *Idlewood* was off to the Balearics to have some work done on its hull; my timing couldn't have been better. So, forty hours later, I'm sailing off into the sunset on this beautiful mega-yacht. It was extraordinary. The kitchen wasn't a galley – it was the size of the kitchen in my house in London, which is to say, massive for a boat. It was all windows and brushed stainless steel. For the shopping, we used a little tender. There were twenty-two crew members, and our salaries were amazing, at least to us. I was earning about $4,000 per month, which is a fortune particularly when you consider that I no longer had any outgoings. You'd go out for a run in the morning, and then come back, pull off your t-shirt and shorts, and they'd be folded and pressed and back on your bed by one o'clock the same afternoon. I didn't even have to cook for the crew; that was the job of my assistant. The lifestyle was just mind-blowing.

It turned out that the boat was owned by Reg Grundy and his wife, Joy Chambers. Reg is one of Australia's most famous media moguls, the founder of the Grundy Organisation, the company responsible for shows like *Young Doctors*, *Sons and Daughters* and, most famously of all, *Neighbours*. Joy is a novelist and an actress (she played Rosemary Daniels in *Neighbours*). They were charming – just the perfect employers and, like Ginger Steve, who was obsessively protective of them, I loved them to bits. I'm still in touch with them. They came to Aubergine when it opened, they came to my wedding and they send my children presents. They were based in Bermuda, but moved around a lot. They spent about three months of every year on board the boat. It must have had an annual budget that ran well into seven figures, irrespective of where it was going – that was just to keep it functioning.

The Grundys didn't join us for the first sixty days or so – they didn't do long journeys on the boat, they would just fly in. I spent nine months on the boat altogether. It was a great life, a seductive life, but nine months is about as long as you can live like that without the dream turning sour. You start to resent the owners, you see. You're living the high life, acting like you're the millionaire, and then they turn up and you find yourself thinking, completely unreasonably, of course: oh, fucking hell, so we've got to do some work now, have we? It was easy to get spoiled – too easy. I remember when I used to go shopping, the crew would all be asking me to get different cereals – Frosties and Coco Pops, or whatever. In the end, I told them they could have cornflakes and nothing more. They were getting too soft, if you ask me.

After the summer season in Europe, the boat used to go back to the Mediterranean. Over this period, I'd saved about £15,000, which seemed like a fortune to me, and I'd been running every day, so I was fit again. I was physically and mentally strong, and I felt fantastic. I'd been to Sardinia and Sicily and Corsica. I'd been through St Tropez twenty times, and Monaco about fifty (that's where the boat was based). I was getting to understand the ins and outs of all the night navigation. I was obsessed with diving, and with waterskiing, which we used to do in the dark, lighting up our path with the searchlights from the boat. But I also knew it had to end; this wasn't the real world. I didn't want to lose sight of reality. However much I was enjoying myself, I was still dying to get back to London and open my own restaurant.

Then I was asked if I would travel with the boat to the Caribbean. The idea was that I would cross the Atlantic in the boat and then the Grundys would pay for me to fly back to Europe from Antigua afterwards. I was tempted. The idea of it appealed to me; when would I get the chance to do something like it ever again? Ginger Steve had never done an Atlantic crossing before, so they had to employ another captain as well for insurance purposes. But Joey, the Australian chief engineer was qualified. He'd done it ten times before, and he was a cool guy – as cool as a cucumber. So I agreed. This would be my final stint on *Idlewood*, but I would do it.

We left Cannes on something like the first of October, and from there we went to Ibiza and then to Gibraltar, where we fuelled up. Then we spent the next eleven days on the Atlantic. I was pretty nervous, especially when I saw the body bags going on the boat, and learned that we were to have a doctor travelling with us. It was then that I realised that there is nothing you can do once you're out at sea – heart attack, ruptured appendix. You have your medical, but it's still a journey and a half. The body bags really put the frighteners on me. We travelled at about nine miles an hour. The waves out there aren't waves, they're big, sweeping rollers. After three days, the wind hit force ten. I was sick as hell, not least because the boat had to be boarded up to make it stormproof, and that only seemed to make us all feel worse. I was practically walking about the place with a bucket 'round my neck. I had the most severe sunburn on the back of my neck because I was permanently hanging over the water, throwing up. It was very lonely. We saw whales, but the only boats were on the radar screen, thirty miles away. No planes flew over. It was just, you know, like the Ancient Mariner – water, water everywhere.

Then something really bizarre happened. Ginger Steve used to drink a lot, and he was only a little man. We were still two days outside of Antigua when he decided to throw a party. It was going to be on the top deck, where there was a five-foot patch of grass specially laid on for the Grundys' dog, Calpernia. How the other half live, eh? The idea was that we would pretend we were on land.

Things were probably already quite tense. There were about ten or eleven of us on board, which is hard: it's almost like being in the *Big Brother* house or something. You start off reasonably lovey-dovey, but that soon changes to something else – irritation, or even hate. You find out a lot about a man when you're stuck out at sea with nothing to do and nowhere to go. We took turns at watch – four hours on and four hours off, and that was tough, too.

So the party kicked off. Ginger Steve made a big bucket of punch, and everyone was having a glass, and the weather was hot and we were all picking up a nice tan. Music was blaring out of a pair of huge speakers – Bob Marley. That's when I started to feel a bit guilty. I thought: we shouldn't really be doing this. The owners would be mortified if they knew. They'd always been so good to us, paying for our travel, telling us to treat ourselves to dinner when we'd worked hard. I felt embarrassed. Then I noticed that Ginger Steve, having been a bit testy with the first officer about how far, precisely, we were from land (he thought a day; the first officer, who knew better, said three), had got his head stuck right inside the bowl of punch. He was incredibly pissed, and now he wanted everyone else to do the same; he thought it would be a funny game. I didn't fancy it at all.

Fifteen minutes later, I was standing right at the very prow of the boat, when Ginger Steve got really violent. I mentioned that he was very protective of our employer. Well, now he took it upon himself to tell me that I'd got to stop talking to the Grundys; I'd got to stop going into the dining room after dinner and meeting their guests and talking about my career. Then he fucking punched me. I pushed him away.

'You're talking shit,' I said. 'You're drunk.'

But as I pushed him away, he punched me again, this time in the face. At this, I snapped. I punched him back. Unfortunately, I knocked him out cold. But when he came round, a few moments later, there was no sign at all that he'd come to his senses: he was more violent than ever. So then it was a case of mutiny on the *Idlewood*. The rest of us had to pin him down, and get him locked safely in his cabin.

When we got to Antigua, he still had a yellow eye.
I looked at it, and I was determined that I would ring
the Grundys and tell them that I wouldn't be staying on
for Christmas. The trouble was, it was so seductive – the
Caribbean. They weren't due to arrive until the twenty-
third of December, which meant that I had plenty of time
to get my advanced diver certificate (I'd learned all the
theory while we were at sea). Plus, even as I packed my
bags, the captain was begging me to stay. He didn't want
the embarrassment of having to tell the Grundys I was
going. So eventually, I calmed down – and, oh God, it was
beautiful: St Barts and St Kitts; we had the most amazing
time. After Christmas, the boat was going up to Fort
Lauderdale, to have some more work done on the hull, and
the Grundys were flying off. I was thinking: this HAS to
be it. I can't do two seasons. It'll do my head in. I'm losing
my touch. I've got all this energy and all these ideas, and
I'm dying to try them out on a wider audience.

What happened next, though, was pure farce. It was
February by this time, and we were in the Virgin Islands.
Ginger Steve got a phone call to say that his father had
taken ill, and he had to fly back to Australia. So the first
officer took over, and he was a bit of a boatie weirdo. He
had an obsession about the watch rota, with making sure
that whoever was on duty put up the 8 a.m. flag. You'd find
him there outside your cabin of a morning, shouting:

'There's one minute to go!' And he had it in for me. I was a chef – I didn't care about his stupid flag; it didn't mean anything to me. We just didn't get on. The trouble was, at that time, he probably didn't know as much as he should have done. Ginger Steve was a control freak, who never taught anyone else how to do anything on board in case they usurped him in some way. We had to move the boat something like eighty-eight metres, and the first officer was in charge, which had never happened before. He weighed anchor. We were moving in because there was a big storm, but the tenders were still out. The Grundys were up on deck playing cards, and I was fishing off the prow, something they encouraged if we were off duty. Suddenly, I heard this terrific bang. The first officer had reversed the yacht over one of the tenders. I ran to the side of the boat, and there it was, sinking fast. Without thinking, I dived in, grabbed one of its ropes in order to try and save it. Grundy went mad, absolutely berserk. He thought it was too dangerous.

'Your life is far more important than some fucking speed-boat,' he said. 'Are you stupid? Just let the boat sink.' Poor Reg. There he was, in his office, thinking: my captain's gone, my first officer can't even pilot the boat, my guests are all up for the weekend – this is bloody embarrassing. Suddenly, I just felt really, really sorry for him. The fact that we hadn't told him all that had happened as we made the big crossing started to bother me even more. I had this sudden urge to tell him the truth. I felt terrible that people were taking advantage of his generosity. So I confessed. Not just about the mini-mutiny, but about the fact that I had discovered that Steve had been taking a backhander – a Harley motorbike, as it happens – from the company in Fort Lauderdale that was going to install an amazing new on-board satellite TV system. Really, he should have asked for a discount, and then passed that on to Mr Grundy. But he didn't – and I'd inadvertently caught sight of the letter thanking him for the business he'd put their way, and confirming the deal he'd struck, on the boat's fax machine. He was in it up to his neck.

Mr Grundy called a big meeting. All the girls on board were bawling their eyes out because they thought they were going to lose their jobs, and it was really sad because he went round us, one by one, getting us to tell him what had happened. By the end, Mr Grundy's jaw was on the floor: his multi-million-pound vessel, and this was what had happened behind his back. But in another way, I felt great. My conscience was clear. At Fort Lauderdale, I would be able to say goodbye to everyone knowing that the slate was clean. Ginger Steve was sacked.

Sadly, a week after he lost his job, Steve went out on his Harley with a drink in him, and drove straight into an articulated lorry. I don't know if it was suicide or an accident. I felt sorry for Reg when I heard this terrible news, but I didn't feel guilty myself, even though it was me who had snitched. I can't feel guilty. I would probably do the same again. At least I think I would.

Cooking for the Grundys helped me to develop my style even further, strange as that may sound. They loved food – they adored fine dining – but they were also health-conscious. Joy was very keen that Reg follow a low-fat diet; she was pretty strict about that, which I found very endearing. So breakfast was stewed fruit, and dinner was very light, no cream, no butter, even if there were ten important guests around the table. For me, it was extra-ordinary; I was being paid very well indeed to evolve my own culinary style. You can see the traces of my time on the *Idlewood* in the way I cook now, no question. There was one night when Joy announced that she had had enough of fine food and wanted something basic and English. She came up with the idea of Shepherd's pie. Brilliant con-cept, of course, except I didn't have a clue how to make it. Fortunately ship-to-shore radios were very much part of this amazing boat and within ten minutes I had located Mum in Bridgwater and she was going through the recipe in five easy stages. Joy, none the wiser as to the real creator of this great dish, announced that it was exactly what she wanted and well done Gordon. What a team!

I had so much respect for Reg. We got on like a house on fire. He was so loyal to his staff, some of whom had worked for him for thirty-five years, and in a way, he taught me the importance of looking after individuals long before I opened the doors of my own restaurant. But that full-time way of life didn't do it for me. Two-thirds of the people who inhabit that world are on the run from real life. If you were a certain kind of guy, you would wait till you were out of your uniform and your employer was on dry land, and then you'd pass the boat off as your own. There were always thirty or so girls outside on the harbour, desperately trying to get in, thinking some footballer or rock star was on board. It was all too easy to pull the wool over these girls' eyes. I think some of the deck hands started to believe their fantasies in the end – they'd lived the lifestyle for so long. Some of these men had persuaded themselves that they owned the boats on which they worked. But not me. I kept my imaginary restaurant – my dream – in my mind's eye at all times. I never let myself forget that this, for me, was just another leg in my journey. And I could feel myself getting closer to achieving it every day. I could almost SMELL that restaurant of mine. It was in my sights. I just had to reach out and grab it with both hands.

CHAPTER SIX
A ROOM OF MY OWN

I GOT A CALL from Pierre Koffmann, the chef and pro-
prietor of La Tante Claire in Chelsea, a restaurant with
three Michelin stars. His head chef had just walked out, and
he wanted to know if I was interested in the job. Of course
I said yes, even though what I was really after was a place of
my own. At the time, La Tante Claire was the envy of every
chef in London – and that included 'my old friend', Marco,
who as soon as he heard I'd accepted a job there, was on
the phone pestering me until one Friday night, after service,
I finally agreed to see him. He said it was urgent, though
with Marco that could mean anything. Basically, he was
pissed off because, the way he saw it, I was just making
Koffmann's life easier for him – too easy, in his view. He
saw Koffmann as a rival, whereas I could only respect him
as a chef.

Marco's star was still very much in the ascendant. He was
going great guns at Harvey's, he was about to move to a

new restaurant in the Hyde Park Hotel. In partnership with Michael Caine, he was involved in The Canteen in Chelsea Harbour, where he'd installed my old flatmate Stephen Terry as chef. Why did I agree to meet him? Simple. He dangled the bait – the biggest bait of all.

'How do you fancy your own restaurant?' he said.

'You know I've always wanted my own fucking restaurant.'

'Well, meet me tonight at ten for dinner.'

I met him at The Canteen, and we jumped in a cab. He wouldn't tell me where we were going, but eventually we wound up in Park Walk. I'd never even heard of fucking Park Walk. Then we walked into this restaurant. It was all galvanised steel and black paint, and it was called Rossmore. When we sat down, Marco said: 'All this can be yours.'

'What the fuck are you on about?' I said.

'The chef's a fucking arsehole,' he said.

I was confused. I'd heard about Rossmore. It had opened about six months before, and it was still being reviewed in the newspapers.

'Yeah, but you can't just give me a restaurant – it's not yours to give.'

'No, but my other partner at The Canteen – he owns it. It's losing ten grand a week.'

A waiter came over to take our order. I was hesitant. Were we going to stay for dinner if Marco was about to stitch the chef up like a piece of best beef fillet? But he had no such qualms. 'Yeah, yeah,' he said. 'Fuck it. We'll eat.' He then ordered one portion of every single thing on the menu.

I'd only been at La Tante Claire for three months. Koffmann was paying me well, which was great, but he was also turning out to be a bit of a handful to work for because my food was now at least as good as his. He never wanted to put my specials on the menu. He wanted his grey mullet and I wanted my red, or my sauce for the grouse was not as strong as his, and we were fighting against each other all the time. So in another way, the idea of escape was quite appealing.

The following week, Marco told me that he'd give me 25 percent of the restaurant, close it down and reopen it a week later. I was horrified. I needed to give Koffmann a month's notice, at least. But he was adamant: it was now or never. Christ, I thought. What do I do? I was still only twenty-six. But I made my mind up quickly. I went to the Midland Bank, borrowed £10,000, and put it into what became Aubergine. Marco had no financial involvement in the deal. He'd just set the whole thing up for his own personal reasons. It was a scary situation. More to the point, I never did see my share certificates. I just got told that they were mine and that was supposed to be enough.

I started on a £22,000 salary, and I was supposed to open the following week. 'Fucking hell,' I said to Marco. 'How am I supposed to open on the first of October when I've got no staff and no menu?'

'Don't worry, don't worry,' he said. 'We'll do one thing at a time. We'll open up as a bistro at first, and we'll cook your desserts in The Canteen.'

It was chaos.

I told Koffmann that I was off. He was, unsurprisingly, mightily pissed off – especially when he realised that I'd be working in Chelsea. Chefs are like dogs – they don't like having a rival on their patch. So he told me to go then and there. This was unnerving: everything seemed to be happening so quickly.

You'll be wondering why I wasn't more wary. I was just excited about having my own place. I didn't ever sit back and think: who's this? What are they up to? A lot of Italians piled in to the deal, but I never questioned their involvement. Just let me cook, I thought. And I was also reassured by the fact that, technically, Marco had no share in the place.

It was all quite hand-to-mouth. These were days when rag-rolling was still the in thing, and I remember mixing yellow paint with a little bit of white and then daubing it on the walls myself. We had a telephone in the bar that you had to put ten pence in to make a call. And because the old restaurant was riddled with debt, we had to put up with that kind of thing. I inherited a mostly Portuguese staff. The first week we were open, I must have sacked about eight of them. They'd stand behind the bar, eating their baguettes. If a customer came in, they'd stick their sandwiches on the bar and wipe their faces with their hands. I couldn't believe it.

But I had a good right-hand man – or at least I did in the end. The day before I left La Tante Claire, Marcus Wareing came in. Marcus is now one of Gordon Ramsay Holdings' big names: he is the chef at *The Savoy Grill*, where he has one Michelin star, and at *Pétrus* at *The Berkeley*, where he now has two stars. He and I had worked together at Le Gavroche, and now he was on the verge of going out to the States to work for Albert there: he was just waiting for his American visa. In this hiatus, he was going to work for Koffmann. I didn't offer him a job myself, although I would have liked to, because I had no money to pay him. I was prepared to be a one-man band, and I worked my nuts off. But occasionally, Marco would come in and help, together with Steve Terry. I'd be on the fish and meat, Marco would be on the sauce and Steve would be on the garnish. It was like the good old days, the three of us working that stove again. It was on one of those nights that Marcus reappeared. He'd just come by to say hello. 'Who the fuck is this?' said Marco, so I told him.

'What the fuck are you at Tante Claire for?' he said to Marcus. 'Learn from this guy (to my amazement, he meant me) – he's just back from Paris and he's got more going for him than you would ever believe. You should be HERE.'

'Yeah, well, I do want a job,' said Marcus.

My ears pricked right up. Fucking hell, I thought. Great. Marcus wants a job. By this point, I was in a better position to pay him.

'I'll give Koffmann a month's notice,' he said.

Marco's reply was predictable. 'Fuck that. You want the job, you start tomorrow.' And, lo and behold, that's what happened. Marcus went in to La Tante Claire early, picked up his knives before Koffmann arrived in the kitchen and was at Aubergine by 7.30 a.m. the next morning. So then there were three – me, Marcus and a sous chef. And later, of course, all the great chefs who are still with me now came through that kitchen: Angela Hartnett, now at *The Connaught*; Mark Sargeant, who is Chef de Cuisine at *Gordon Ramsay at Claridge's*; and Mark Askew, who is Head Chef at *Royal Hospital Road* and Executive Chef at Gordon Ramsay Holdings. I didn't know it at the time, but Aubergine turned out to be the greatest training ground for chefs in Britain.

Meanwhile, my private life was getting tricky. The owners of Aubergine – the mysterious Italians – had a flat in South Kensington, and Ros and I set up home there. We decided to give it one more go. In fact, we decided to get engaged, which was fucking stupid. 'I'm coming back to the UK, I want some form of commitment from you,' she said. 'I'm not going to jack in my job in Paris and come back and support you again if you're not going to commit.'

She pointed out that I still owed her quite a lot of money, and that her credit-card bill was somewhat on the hefty side. Fair enough, I thought. So, like a fool, I said: 'Well, let's get engaged.' Oh, fuck.

Our 'engagement' lasted all of six months. The pressure I was under at the time was fucking extraordinary. Madness at work, and then a date set for a wedding. It was so claustrophobic. I was working myself half to death during the week and then, on a Sunday, I'd be practically comatose. I didn't want to get up and go shopping and this, that and the other. Was I selfish? Yes, I was fucking selfish. This was my one chance to climb the ladder. Things came to a head one day after a really shit service. A cook had failed to show up that day, and Ros had asked me to meet her at four o'clock at the church in Chelsea so we could talk to the vicar about the church and the ceremony. Well, I'd had the service from hell. I saw the clock. It was five minutes to four, but I wasn't in a hurry – the church was only fifty yards from Aubergine's door, after all. But she wasn't taking any chances. I heard Jean-Claude, my maître d', say my name, and I turned round, and there she was. The walk to the vicarage felt like the death march to me. When we got there, I just sat there like a fucking zombie while the vicar talked about the importance of attending church, and how it might be a good idea if we didn't have children straight away so we could enjoy our life together. I just looked at him. Eventually, Ros said, 'Are you all right?' I told her that I was fine, that I'd just had a terrible service, but that was the moment when I knew – I was making a huge mistake.

That night, after service, I went home determined to get it over with straight away. I told her that I was under pressure, more hard up than ever, and that the whole idea of marriage was a bad one. Whatever I owed her on the credit card, the truth was that I was finding it impossible to cook at the very highest level and have a relationship. She went fucking mad.

I felt relieved, but it wasn't over then. In the build-up to our so-called wedding, I'd bought her an Old English Sheepdog called Ben. The idea was that he would comfort her since I was away six nights a week. So, when Ros kicked me out and I got a flat above her, she didn't just make me pay both lots of rent and the credit-card bills, she made me pay for the dog's keep and walk him every day. In other words, I was getting further and further in the shit. She was an amazing woman, and I'd fancied the pants off her when I first met her back at Le Gavroche – but there was an age gap between us that just became too difficult. Some days, I wanted to go wild. I didn't want to sit in, knitting and planning for a family. I wanted to go out and do something to clear my mind. She was articulate, clever, very proper, but I was far more excited about cooking than I was about being with her. In the end, home seemed like a more stressful option than the kitchen.

Or maybe she just wasn't the right woman for me. Because it wasn't long after we split up that I met Tana, who is now my wife and the mother of our four children. Tana was going out with a friend of mine, Tim Powell, who had also worked at Tante Claire. This was in 1993–4. Not long after we'd opened Aubergine, Tim and Tana came in for dinner with Tana's parents, Chris and Greta Hutcheson (Chris is now the CEO of Gordon Ramsay Holdings, so I think it's fair to say that I owe him more than just my wife). God, I thought, there's my mate with that stunning girlfriend of his, whom I'd met briefly a year ago when he picked me up at an airport. At the time, I remember saying to Tim: 'How does someone fat and bald like you pull such an amazing girl?' But six months after that, he'd called me to tell me that he was engaged to her. Fucking great, I thought. I was incredibly pissed off.

That evening, I didn't get to speak to them much. I just remember Tim acting all brash and cocky, showing off to his future father-in-law. But I gave them all a glass of champagne and then I cooked my heart out. I wanted to make a point because by then, he was working for Terence Conran at Le Pont de la Tour, a restaurant more famous for its ashtrays than for its food. No disrespect, but you don't go to bloody Terence Conran for fine dining. You might go to him for a sofa, but you don't go to him for an experience in food. I remember going to Mezzo for dinner once. It was like being in a Ford car plant. The food was on an assembly line, and it tasted like it. I wanted to confirm to Tim that while he was cutting langoustines in half and dipping them in fucking lemongrass mayonnaise, or flash-frying a steak on a grill, I'm busting my nuts with the most amazing ravioli of lobster and tournedos of beef.

Then Tana had a New Year's Eve party, to which I was invited. And there Tim was, telling me how his future father-in-law was going to set him up in a restaurant. So now, I was getting even more pissed off. The restaurant in question is now the Midsummer House in Cambridge, which is one of the best in the country, and has two Michelin stars – though that's nothing to do with Tim.

Meanwhile, I'm tied up with a bunch of Italians that I'm not quite sure of. Anyway, I'm at this party, and this guy corners me. I'd only been there for five minutes and he's going on about how arrogant I was, how I should learn not to be so cocky. 'You may cook,' he said. 'But you've got to learn a bit about life.' This man turned out to be Chris Hutcheson again – the future father-in-law.

He had me pressed right against the wall. All of a sudden, though, a fight kicked off. It seemed that Tim had taken it upon himself to fight Tana's brothers. This was great news. Tee hee. I was hopeful that the little squirt would be really in the shit now.

But, not a bit of it.

It must have been about three months later when I heard that Chris had sent Tim off to New York for work experience with Daniel Boulud. I couldn't believe my ears: the little bastard was getting everything that I ever wanted, big-time. I buried myself in my work. As well as Aubergine, I started doing development work with Marks & Spencer – a bit of consultancy behind the scenes. I needed the money. Ros's rent was £1,200 a month and my shitty little studio flat cost me another £800. The only relief I could get from all the worry was my Yamaha motorbike. It was my fucking man machine. On a Saturday night, I'd go down to Bar Italia in Soho and meet all my mates, and then we'd all pile out on to the M4, where we'd sit on our petrol tanks and play dare to see who could hold it at full throttle, and keep it there from bridge to bridge. Whoever funked it paid for all the espressos and cappuccinos back at Bar Italia. We used to do it until about five in the morning, when the roads were completely clear and the sun was just coming up, one lane each. I never lost. I wouldn't drop the throttle – that rush of clinging on to the petrol tank and the vibration of this fucking thing between your thighs and thinking that at any minute a Coke can or a conker would come your way and make you fly – it was an unbelievable adrenalin rush, and the only possible way I could relax after service.

I couldn't afford to park this bike anywhere, but Tim and Tana had this amazing penthouse in one of the loft buildings above Conran's Le Pont de la Tour restaurant in Butler's Wharf, and Tim had said that I could park my bike in his garage there. It must have been early summer, June, when I went down there in the small hours of the morning to get my bike. I buzzed the door of the flat, and Tana answered. I'd assumed that she would be in bed. I'd left my keys at their place in case Tim had to move the bike during the week.

'Where's Tim?' I said.

'Didn't you know? Tim and I separated a week ago.'

'You're joking!' I said. I tried to seem sympathetic, but inside I was dancing a jig.

So, boom! I was straight upstairs. I didn't bother going to Soho to see my mates. Instead, I stayed with her, talking, until about six in the morning. It was great! We were having such a laugh. Apparently, Tim had met some waitress in New York – Tana had found some kind of evidence in his pocket and kicked him out. Then I asked her if she fancied coming out on the bike, riding pillion with me. Tim had his own helmet somewhere. So, as dawn broke, we set off. On the way, we had to be careful to dodge the building's CCTV cameras – we left separately and she met me a hundred metres down the road, because her Dad lived right at the top of the building in another penthouse. He knew the security guards: he would see me with Tana, and we didn't want that – not just yet.

So that was how we started seeing each other, though

we both kept our own flats on for the first six months. We married in December 1996. Why did Tana succeed where Ros had failed? I think because, at first at least, we were just having fun. There was no pressure; we weren't scrutinising each other's every move. So it didn't feel claustrophobic. We didn't have everything all mapped out. Tana was studying to be a nursery teacher, and working as her father's PA and then going to night school, so there were very few times when we could see each other, in any case. Mondays to Saturdays were completely out. Plus, she knew what it meant to be driven, to be obsessed with your work – she'd seen the same trait in her father. When she was growing up, he sometimes used to work twenty-four hours a day. So I never had to account for my movements to her, and I was grateful for that.

CHAPTER SEVEN

WAR

WE GOT OUR first Michelin star at Aubergine fourteen months after we opened our doors, in 1995. I was still only twenty-eight years old. I got my first star, and Marco got his third. Two years later, in 1997, we got our second. So we went from nothing at all to two stars in just three years; the only other restaurant that had ever achieved this was Harvey's. Every one came: Princess Margaret, David Bowie, Robert de Niro. We were so busy not even Madonna could get a table. At this point, things started to get interesting.

It was around now that my relationship with the Italians – Claudio Pulse and my other partners, Giuliano Lotto and Franco Zanellato – began to get difficult. My relationship with Marco also started to go the same way.

A few months after I got my first star, Marco told me that he needed to talk to me.

'My chef is leaving,' he said. 'I'm going to give you a share of my business, I'm going to make you my best of chefs, and I'm going to pay you £100,000 a year; you'll never need to worry about money again. Don't tell me now. I want you to think about it. Let's have dinner on Sunday night.'

Fuck me.

That Sunday, over dinner I told him. 'That's an amazing offer,' I said. 'The thought of running your three-star restaurant is a huge honour. But I was with you at Harvey's when you got those two stars and, to be honest, all I want to do now is win two stars myself.'

His reaction was immediate, and shocking – even though I had more experience than most of his temper. He didn't bother trying to persuade me that I was wrong. He took it personally. Unwittingly, I had crossed a line that I hadn't even known was there.

'You're fucking MAD,' he said. Whereupon he started raving on about the inside story of my Italian business partners, including how much debt they were in and what their plans were for Aubergine. Jesus Christ. All I'd done was turn down his fucking job.

'They're about to pull the plug,' he said. 'They're going to sell the restaurant, and you haven't got a pot to piss in.'

So I went to Claudio. The place was fully booked, we were taking forty grand a week at least; weren't we secure?

'We're not making any money, Gordon,' he said.

'I know, but we've got good cash flow. It's a healthy business.'

Then he gave his side of the story so far as Marco went. Things had started to go sour over at The Canteen. Michael Caine wanted the restaurant to keep it simple, to serve fish and chips, decent steaks. But Marco wanted to push the boundaries a little . . .

Not long after this, Marco quit The Canteen. So, although I hated being piggy in the middle so far as The Canteen went – after Marco's exit, I sometimes had to help out in the kitchen there, advising on menus and so on – I relaxed a little. It seemed to me that Aubergine was safe for now.

Even so, at that time paranoia had started to kick in and I was convinced that Marco was trying to get back at me for turning down his offer. When Aubergine picked up an unexpectedly bad review – it was by Jonathan Meades in *The Times* – I was convinced that he was some-how behind it. Ditto a horrible review by A. A. Gill, the restaurant critic of the *Sunday Times*. I knew that Gill and Marco went shooting together, they are best buddies to this day, so it was easy to convince myself that they were in cahoots. Would Marco have arranged for the two most famous restaurant critics in Britain to fuck me over? I really do not know. In a way, it is funny now: the stuff they were writing was so obviously rubbish. But still, I felt vulnerable and twitchy and very, very nervous. I can now see with hindsight that I was probably just being neurotic.

Then, out of the blue, Claudio told me that he and the others wanted to open a second fine-dining restaurant. Again, they would give me a 10 percent share. All I had to do was find a chef. I immediately thought of Marcus Wareing, whom I'd just sent off to Paris. So he came back, and we opened L'Oranger in St James's – it was a huge success. Even A. A. Gill liked it. It won a Michelin star after just six months.

The Italians offered to convert my shares in Aubergine and L'Oranger into a share of the restaurant group as a whole. At the time, this seemed a generous offer, and I accepted. The group was turning over plenty of cash.

So my restaurant was turning about £2 million a year and even L'Oranger, a relative baby, was turning about £2.5 million a year. If you looked at the talent we were nursing, we were just getting stronger and stronger. But then the partners started talking about bistros and brasseries and even a pizza joint, of rolling out more and more restaurants, all Aubergine-inspired, and I started to get nervous. It felt like the management was all over the place. They didn't know what they were doing. I wasn't into cloning myself. I was into excellence, and control.

The next thing that happened was that other companies started sniffing round with a view to buying us. Luke Johnson, the man behind Pizza Express, was interested, and so was Virgin. These guys in suits would show up and

I would have to appear excited and enthusiastic when I wasn't really interested in selling my share at all, for all that I was offered £1.5m for it at one point. I had a word with my father-in-law. I told him that I thought Claudio would sell out regardless of my feelings, and offer me as part of the package. What was I to do? In my contract, it said that if I left the group, I wasn't allowed to open a new restaurant within a twenty-five-mile radius of Aubergine. Chris advised me not to sign anything.

My only power lay in the fact that I owned 10 percent of the company. But it turned out that my little share was not quite as crucial as I had imagined. Claudio and Franco had 22.5 percent each, and Giuliano had 45 percent. At this point, my relationship with the Italians went downhill fast. I had a phone call from my pastry chef. 'Gordon,' he said. 'I've just been talking with Marco, and he was asking me lots of questions about you. He wanted to know how many hours you were working, how many nights a week you're there. And in his office, there were copies of all the menus from Aubergine and L'Oranger.'

What had happened was this: Giuliano and Franco had realised I wasn't interested in signing anything – least of all an agreement that if I sold my shares, I could stay on as a consultant – so now they were lining up Marco as a consultant. They were going to use him as a stick to beat me. The plan was to tell me that if I didn't sign the contract, and they didn't sell the group, I'd be out anyway, to be replaced by Marco. Marco, of course, denied this. Claudio, meanwhile, told me to keep calm – that if we stuck together there was no need to worry because, between us, we had a good share of the business, irrespective of what Giuliano and Franco did. But what I didn't know is that the bastard was on the verge of selling his shares to Giuliano – who wouldn't need my shares then anyway. I was going to get fucked either way. He was selling me up the fucking Swanee. How did I discover all this? I had my own spy, as it happens.

I had a call, cloak-and-dagger style. 'Watch your back,' said the voice on the end of the line. 'Don't trust any of them because they're all bastards, they're all out to screw each other, and there's a massive fucking deal going on. They're about to sell the company, and they're going to sell you with it. Don't listen to Giuliano, and don't listen to Claudio, and stay away from Marco.' Then the person hung up.

A lot of rumours were swirling about the London restaurant world – like steam over a pan of stock. 'Aubergine's going to be taken over by Marco Pierre White,' people were saying, or 'Gordon's about to lose his two stars'. Marco was delighted. Victory, at last.

I was 31 years old, Tana had just got pregnant with our first baby, I'd got myself a fucking new mortgage and I was up to my fucking eyeballs in debt. Basically, I was totally in the shit. I'd created this phenomenal restaurant, and I'd nearly killed myself doing it, and now it was about to be taken away from me.

So, I did the craziest thing I have ever done. The night I came up with my masterplan, I couldn't sleep, so I went up to a little café by Chelsea bridge and got myself a cup of coffee and a bacon sandwich, and I sat there all night plotting how I could secure my bollocks. What I needed was an idea which would turn the Italians against Marco. That way all their plans would crumble to dust. And I needed to keep my own nose clean, for the time being at least.

Marco had been my mentor, but I had outgrown him. Now I was the threat. I had two Michelin stars and he could see I was within sight of my third. I knew he could not live with that. Well, there was no way I was going to allow him to take away everything I had worked for year after year, sixteen hours a day, six days a week. Although I was young, 31, I was not going to roll over just because it was Marco. There was no way I would let him take away my family's lifeline.

By morning, I had it. I would organise the disappearance of the reservation book and to the Italians, at least, I would make it clear that its disappearance was the work of Marco.

In the days before computers and the internet, a top restaurant's reservations book was its greatest asset, worth its weight in gold. We were fully booked between four and six months in advance, and the book had details of every single one of those bookings. Without it, the place would descend into total chaos. So that's precisely what happened. I made it disappear.

Pandemonium ensued. Needless to say, the news of the disappearance spread like wildfire. We were inundated with calls from punters who didn't actually have reservations, but who were happy to try it on knowing the mess we were in. As for the newspapers, they were avid for details, and I was all too happy to do as many interviews as they wanted. 'Only someone in the trade would know the full value of a reservations book,' I told journalists.

The Italians, meanwhile, were in deep shock. They were starting to get really panicky. Even though Marco denied his involvement, he couldn't actually prove it – and besides, who else would want our reservations book? 'He thinks he is going to get control of the restaurant anyway,' I told them. 'This is just him getting ahead of himself as usual.' But the thing that really convinced them that the skulduggery was all his was when the previous night's reservations, photocopied from the book, mysteriously started being faxed through to Aubergine. Sometimes it arrived from a Kall Kwik near to one of Marco's restaurants. It worked like a treat.

Where did I keep the diary during all this? Oh, I had it in a very safe place.

It now looked less and less as if Marco would be taking over any time soon. The Italians were unbelievably pissed off with him. In fact, they were right back on my side. I was relieved. If Marco had taken over, all I had worked for would have been lost. It wasn't just that I no longer liked the man, I no longer trusted him to act in my best interests.

At the end of 1997, I'd been approached by David Levin, the owner of The Greenhouse, who was looking to replace Gary Rhodes, who'd just left. Levin had made what seemed like a very generous offer to me of a salary of £150,000 a year and a 5 percent share of the business. Levin also owned The Capital, one of London's finest restaurants, so the idea of working for him had seemed very attractive to me. Unlike the Italians, who seemed, at bottom, uninterested in the idea of fine dining, Levin knew all about it; he also knew that, correctly managed, excellent restaurants could make as much money as pasta joints.

However, in the end, I'd refused his offer, in spite of the fact that the prospect of working at The Greenhouse involved considerably less risk than the idea of opening up on my own. Why? Simple. I'd arranged for my father-in-law to have lunch with Levin and he'd come away from that meeting – how shall I put this – somewhat unimpressed. Our big problem with the Italians had always been that they didn't have my best interests, my welfare, at heart – and Chris worried that with Levin I might be dealing with more of the same.

Still, Levin had drawn up a contract, and Chris and I were called to a meeting at his lawyers, Withers, to look at it – or so we thought. To our amazement, this turned out to be a completion meeting rather than a discussion of my future. Levin, meanwhile, didn't even turn up, sending his son, Joe, as his proxy (daddy was playing golf, we gathered). I felt my father-in-law kick me a couple of times during this meeting until, finally, he asked if we could be excused for a couple of minutes. Outside, Chris looked at me and said: 'What is it that you really want, Gordon?'

'A three-star restaurant,' I said.

'Well no such establishment exists where the chef owns only 5 percent of it,' he said.

We made our excuses and left. I suppose this offer, and Chris's attitude to it, had helped me to get things clear in my head. It was my own place, or nothing. Full steam ahead.

Now that Marco was in bad odour with the Italians, and I knew that escape was on the horizon, I was able to treat Marco the same way he'd treated me: I could string him along. Luckily, and not for the first time, Marco now needed me, which meant I could bide my time while the escape plan I was working on came to fruition. He was in the middle of a massive feud with Tony Allan, the fishmonger and later the owner of the chain of restaurants called Fish! Tony had been reported as saying that he had once seen Marco put pen ink in his squid ink risotto. Marco had decided to sue, and he needed me as a witness. So he started being nice all of sudden. So, everything was sweet. No point rocking the boat until the time was absolutely right.

By this time, too, Marco had taken over the restaurant at the Café Royal; he now had this idea that he would go into partnership with Chris and me and hand us the Café Royal. We went along with it. What he didn't know was we were in the middle of our own negotiations – to buy the site of La Tante Claire from Pierre Koffmann, who was moving his restaurant to *The Berkeley* in Knightsbridge. The trouble was that his move had been delayed by six months, as *The Berkeley*, part of the Savoy Group, was involved in a massive takeover of Blackstone, the New York-based Private Equity Company, so I had to keep everyone sweet for rather longer than I had expected. It was tricky: like holding a baby and chopping an onion at the same time. Whenever Marco brought up the subject of the Café Royal, I'd smile innocently, and make vaguely enthusiastic noises. And whenever the Italians brought up the subject of my contract with them, I'd smile sweetly and tell them that I just needed to run the whole thing past my lawyers. The smirk on my face must have been a mile wide, we had secured funding for *Royal Hospital Road* and unbeknownst to anyone else, we were on our way to the real start line. Ironically it was also the first time we had heard the name 'Blackstone' which was later to fly us to the stars.

In the end, although I was never called I would have testified for Marco. I had my reasons. It certainly had nothing to do with his arse-kissing – or even to do with the fact that I didn't actually think he would do something as stupid as put ink in risotto nero. Apart from anything else, it would stain the customer's teeth. Basically, I agreed to give evidence for him if he did the same for me. He said that the Italians had approached him to stitch me up – information I thought might come in rather handy at some point.

If I ever needed reminding that I was doing the right thing in escaping Marco's clutches once and for all, it came during a conversation we had outside The Mirabelle in Mayfair, which he had opened only a couple of weeks before. It was astonishing, and involved Jean-Christophe Novelli, a man who Marco probably thinks should be in his eternal debt. Marco was dying to get his hands on Les Saveurs, in Curzon Street, another restaurant which had the same Japanese owners as Mirabelle. At which point, he decided to install Novelli as chef. Novelli had a small chain of bistro-type restaurants which were incredibly successful, but now he wanted to move into fine dining as well. He wanted to go for a few Michelin stars. So Marco installed him at Les Saveurs. I did not believe that Novelli was up to it at that time – and later, I was proved right. He soon lost the Michelin star he'd inherited, and in a period of about six months after that, his other businesses sank without trace, one by one. I should not have been surprised when his 'plate throwing' performance on *Hell's Kitchen* failed to revive his fortunes. But that's another story.

In the garden of the Mirabelle that night, I asked Marco

why on earth he had put Novelli into Les Saveurs. At first, he said nothing; he simply stared at me. His eyes were like the barrels of a gun. His answer, when it came, chilled me.

'Gordon,' he said. 'Gordon. Gordon.'

I waited. He was always one for the high drama.

Then he said: 'Novelli is getting too big for his boots. I don't want him climbing out of his pram, do I?'

CHAPTER EIGHT

THE GREAT
WALK-OUT

I SURVIVED THOSE six months, but barely. Looking back, I'm still not quite sure how. Without telling me, Franco and Claudio had sold their shares in the company to Giuliano, which meant that he now had 90 percent of the business. In other words, he owned it: I didn't matter to him at all. His manner became very forceful. 'We're going to open seven days a week,' he started saying. 'We're going to put up prices.' He had no feel for running restaurants at all. At least Claudio and Franco were restaurateurs by trade; Giuliano was a former stockbroker. There was even talk of a bistro in Bermuda.

He also wanted Jean-Claude to go off and manage Memories of China, and he wanted my sous chef to go and help out in Spighetta (both were other restaurants in the group). My staff were no longer my own, it seemed. Gone were the days when he asked me to do something; now, he simply told me. I didn't like his manner at all. But the one thing he had failed to do was tie me down contractually. I still hadn't signed anything. This turned out to be a fatal error on his part.

Finally, the deal on *Royal Hospital Road* was closed – secretly, of course.

It was a huge relief: I wasn't sure how much longer I could keep massaging Giuliano's hefty ego. The amount of money I'd borrowed was a huge worry, of course, but the move was certainly made easier by a gesture of extraordinary generosity by my old boss, Pierre Koffmann, who agreed that the £500,000 that I was to pay him for the lease on the La Tante Claire property could be made in two instalments. I was to pay him £375,000 now and a further £125,000 a year later. This was fucking decent of him. I mean very, very decent, and I will always be grateful to him for it. It meant that we would have spare cash to revamp the place, establish a decent wine list, recruit staff, and generally get the whole shebang off to a good start.

I felt unbelievably excited. And now, it was time for me to get round to resigning as a director. This should have been fairly straightforward: you know – hand in notice, work out notice, shake hands, piss off. But, thanks mostly to Giuliano, it turned into one of the most dramatic, and infamous, moments in my career so far.

A small discrepancy had been discovered in the food costs at L'Oranger. Meanwhile, the company wanted Marcus to sign a four-year deal tying him to the group as a way of reassuring investors. So far, he had refused; he wasn't keen on the direction the company was now taking either. When this so-called discrepancy was found, Giuliano had an excuse to turn on Marcus.

'Sign this fucking deal, or I'm going to sack you,' he said.

Marcus was unruffled. 'Well, first of all, if I sign, I'd like to see the certificate for my 10 percent share in the company, which I was offered four years ago, and on which I still haven't laid my eyes,' he said.

Marcus is from Liverpool. He's a straightforward kind of a guy.

But, nothing doing. One Friday night, not long after, Giuliano came to me and told me that if Marcus didn't sign the contract that very evening, he would sack him in the morning. 'Are you mad?' I said. 'You're going to sack the head chef?'

Giuliano was about to make the biggest mistake of his life – and, as a shareholder, unfortunately, I had to accompany him to L'Oranger to watch him make it. I made my position as bystander clear to the staff. 'I've no part in this,' I said. 'He's the largest shareholder. But I do have to stand here and witness it.'

Giuliano turned to Marcus, and said: 'Your share has just gone down by 2 percent, and I'm going to sack you if you don't sign this deal.'

'Well, I'm not signing it. So sack me.'

Marcus was duly sacked, and marched off the premises.

Shortly afterwards, Giuliano left the building, at which point I gathered all of the staff around me, both from L'Oranger and Aubergine, and told them that I was going to stand by Marcus. I was leaving, resigning as a director, and I was going to open a new restaurant. 'You're more than welcome to come and join me,' I said. 'I hope there'll be a job there for all of you, but at the moment, nothing is certain. I'm leaving because I'm not happy with the direction this business is going in. If you want to hand in your notice and follow me, that's up to you. Personally, I can't tell you what's going to happen next, though in my view both Aubergine and L'Oranger are finished for good.' Angela was there, Sarge was there, Mark Askew was there. All of us had tears in our eyes.

'My fucking right-hand man has been sacked,' I went on. 'He's sweated his bollocks off for this company for the last five years, and I won't have it.' What happened next was amazing, though it didn't, if I am truthful, surprise me.

I have always had a loyal staff – whatever rubbish used to get printed about my abilities as boss, the ludicrous allegations that I am a bully – and I knew that once I had left the building, Giuliano would be lucky to hang on even to the humblest kitchen porter. But even so, it was immensely touching.

On the spot, forty-six members of staff walked out, and in doing so, effectively closed down two of London's best restaurants.

Both Aubergine and L'Oranger were shut for several weeks while Giuliano frantically tried to get new staff, which meant that the company was losing an awful lot of money (both restaurants turned over £100,000 a week between them). This had a knock-on effect, annoying customers with existing reservations who took their business elsewhere, while other potential customers, quite understandably, had no interest in eating in either place if their acclaimed chefs were no longer in the kitchen. Those restaurants WERE Marcus and me; it was a nonsense to think they could replace us without anyone noticing. Giuliano was incredibly naïve to think he could pull that one off.

Of course, the slight hitch was that I was tied to a notice period. I had to stick around for four weeks, irrespective of what my staff did. Or at least, I had to be SEEN to stick around, for legal reasons. As soon as Giuliano had found out that the staff had gone, he was right back in my face. 'Gordon, you can't do this to me,' he said. 'This is ridiculous.' The guy was bawling his eyes out.

'Listen, mate,' I said. 'What I can do is cook for a table of four on my own, and I can open for lunch and dinner until I leave. I'm resigning as director, but as a chef, I'll be here for another month. What I can't guarantee is that I can run the restaurant at full capacity, or that I can deal with L'Oranger at the same time. Four covers are about your lot.' It was hilarious, really – the utter seriousness with which I told him I would be able to cook for a table of four. You see, he couldn't straightforwardly blame me for the walk-out, whatever he felt in his gut, because I was still standing there. I was fucking standing strong, waving my flag. He must have sensed that I was behind what had happened, but he had no evidence, and my behaviour now was, well, it was impeccable. I might have been taking the piss, but I was also sticking to the letter of the law.

Naturally, the press had a field day. As soon as the news of what had happened got out, the telephones went mad. Every journalist in London wanted the scoop. By the evening, there were TV camera crews on the street outside. The London *Evening Standard* had the story on its billboards – and we still have a copy on prominent display in our head office – 'Staff Walk Out in Protest at Chef's Sacking'. For Giuliano, it was the worst possible kind of publicity.

The next few days were pretty strange. Giuliano told me to get in some agency staff. Meanwhile, he started bringing chefs round – chefs who had the gall to think that they could run Aubergine. Looking at most of them, the very idea was laughable – insulting, even. I used to stand on the stairs and watch them troop in, my jaw swinging in amazement. Even David Cavalier came for a look. (He was clearly in a different league to the other candidates, as he used to be at L'Escargot, and later had his own place, Cavalier's where he'd also won a Michelin star.) When he saw that I was still sitting there, he could hardly believe it. I showed him round myself. He was soon seething, frothing at the mouth – I made it clear that the restaurant hadn't paid any of its creditors for months. Aubergine was a cash cow, and the company had made sure that they had used it as much as they possibly could to fund other parts of the business, knowing that, because it was so famous and obviously successful, creditors were likely to take their time before they came knocking on the door.

As I handed my resignation in, Giuliano was still insisting that we could work things out. But I'd waited eighteen months to have my say, and I wasn't having any of it. 'Don't you know how hard I've been working over the last fucking year?' I said. 'My wife was pregnant with our first child, and we had all sorts of complications and difficulties with that, and all that time you were trying to undermine me. I swear to God, under no circumstances would I ever even think of doing business with you ever again. Now, you clearly own these restaurants. Fuck off and run them!'

I must have made for quite a terrifying sight: my eyeballs were out on stalks, my veins pulsating like I was about to explode. As for his eyes, they were filling up. I thought about all the corporate entertaining he'd done, all the bigwigs he'd brought in, all the money-men I'd impressed on his behalf with my cooking and my profits. It's time for you to learn a few lessons, I thought. The hard way.

A few weeks later, on the first of September 1998, we

opened the doors of Gordon Ramsay *Royal Hospital Road*, on the site of the old La Tante Claire. I found jobs for every single person who'd supported Marcus and me.

It was thrilling. But our troubles weren't over yet.

Giuliano was determined that someone would pay for what had happened at Aubergine and L'Oranger – and that someone, as it turned out, was me. Being issued with a writ is never what you'd call pleasant, but this one's arrival coincided with the funeral of my father. I received it, by hand, on my way back from burying him. I was outside my house, and the two guys were waiting for me.

He was going to sue me for a lot of money. He also accused me of breaking my employment contract by poaching staff.

I was determined to fight it all the way, even though I had no spare cash for legal fees. I was running a new restaurant. New restaurants eat cash, so I had no liquid assets whatsoever. But Giuliano could have his day in court if that was what he wanted. I was happy to oblige. That's not to say that I wasn't shitting myself. On paper, it looked like he might have a strong case.

The writ wasn't only about getting revenge for what had happened after the great walk-out. Giuliano was also furious that we were planning on opening our own second restaurant just a few doors up from L'Oranger. It became *Pétrus*. Marcus was head chef. We were able to take over the lease because things were going so well at *Royal Hospital Road*; we already had double the turnover that Koffmann had produced in the same space.

In the January after we opened, Aubergine lost one of its stars and Gordon Ramsay *Royal Hospital Road* gained two (as a footnote, it might be worth mentioning that when La Tante Claire moved to *The Berkeley*, it lost its third star – though I didn't especially take any pleasure in that, given what Koffmann had done for me). Anyway, Giuliano didn't like it one bit that Marcus was on his territory.

Anyone who wonders just how stressful this period in my life was has only to dig out some old footage of the Channel 4 series, *Boiling Point*, which was filmed around this time. A production company had approached me when I was still at Aubergine about taking part in a series in which a fly-on-the-wall camera would follow a leading chef in his kitchen – in other words, it covered the period just before and just after the split. (This was another thing I'd got over on Marco; he was one of the many names they considered before choosing me.)

The series, my first appearance on TV, was a hit, but it was also extremely controversial. Viewers complained – in their dozens – about both my liberal use of the f-word, and about the way I treated my staff. They accused me of being a bully. They, and some professional organisations, said that it would put young men and women off the idea of the kitchen as a career. I'm sure it wouldn't seem so shocking now – it's thanks to shows like *Boiling Point*, and *Hell's Kitchen*, that the public has come to understand how tough it is working in a professional kitchen. But back then, the public knew nothing; they imagined chefs to be ponces with stupid French accents and big white hats. Then again, perhaps I WAS a little out of control. The pressure must, at some level, have got to me. I remember when I saw the first part of the series myself, in a little screening room – even I was shocked. They'd got some great footage but, seeing myself on screen for the first time, I thought: fucking hell, is that really me? My language was terrible; Mum was appalled.

Afterwards, I didn't turn up to any more viewings. I couldn't face it. As for my father-in-law, I found out later that he had had to have a stiff drink before he watched each weekly episode. We soon had the Bank of Scotland, who'd loaned us so much money, on the telephone asking if I was in danger of over-exposing myself. Well, that was how they put it. What they really meant was: who is this psycho to whom we've just given half a million quid?

It did, however, have a good effect on business. The phones were soon smoking; 50 percent of the callers were saying: how can you be such an arsehole? The other 50 percent were saying: if that's how passionate you are about food, we want to come and eat with you.

Still, I couldn't have gone on like that forever. As Chris

told me at the time, I had to learn to control my temper, to stay cool under pressure, otherwise I was going to kill myself or someone else. I also needed to stop comfort eating, and get fit again. In the first few months at *Royal Hospital Road*, my weight swelled to more than seventeen-and-a-half stone. That's another way you can tell how stressed I felt. When I look at pictures of myself, I'm appalled. I look disgusting: fat and pasty and as under the cosh as any man could ever be.

But back to the writ. First of all, I had to make sure that I had enough cash to fight the case. The only asset I had was our house, so that had to go, and we moved back into rented accommodation. That was a terrible thing to have to do.

My childhood had made me long for a safe, secure home of my own – and no sooner had I got myself one than I had to get rid of it. Plus, I felt terrible for Tana. She comes from a nice, close middle-class family. She had been educated privately. She had been used to a certain way of life. Plus she had Megan, our new baby. It really hurt to have to tell her that we were moving again, and this time we were going back down the property ladder rather than up.

Between shifts at *Royal Hospital Road*, I spent a lot of time with my counsel. He told me that the case was going to be extremely tricky to win. But I did have one ace up my sleeve. I was still a shareholder; I still had my 10 percent. He figured that the whole thing could be put to bed simply because they wanted my shares. Also, as a shareholder, why would I have wanted to damage my own business? That wouldn't have been entirely in my own interests.

In the end, Giuliano didn't get his day in court. In a court management hearing, the judge strongly advised us to settle out of court; it was going to be extremely expensive for both parties if we carried on. In his opinion, even the winner wouldn't walk away with very much. He also warned that, whatever happened, there was no way that I was going to stop cooking; it wasn't possible to stop me. So, four months after I received the writ, we settled out of court. The terms of our agreement have never been revealed, though I think I can say that I was left with a hefty legal bill at the end of it all. I used to joke to the press at the time that I couldn't discuss details because, every time I did, my doorstep would be decorated with horses' heads. I was joking, but I stand by the sentiment. Giuliano was a vengeful man. At the time, I couldn't afford to continue fighting him. I needed to concentrate on my restaurant, and on *Pétrus*. We were on our way now, and we couldn't afford to let anything else stand in our way. Plus, as usual, I was broke.

CHAPTER NINE

THE SWEET SMELL OF SUCCESS

IN JANUARY 2001, *Royal Hospital Road* picked up its third Michelin star – the same day as my wife handed me the keys to a blue Ferrari 550 Maranello. Lovely as the car was, there is no doubt in my mind which was the greater prize. I'd longed for that third star with every sinew for so long, and now all my hard work had paid off: this was the ultimate accolade, the definitive recognition. It also meant, officially, that my restaurant was the best in London because, after a row with the Michelin organisation the previous year, Marco Pierre White and Nico Ladenis both lost their three star status. To this day, mine is still the only three-Michelin-starred restaurant in London.

Of course, chefs periodically slag off Michelin, claiming that it is only interested in overly fussy food; that it doesn't understand any other kind of cuisine but French; that its inspectors are too set in their ways, too obsessed with the intricacies of service, or how chi-chi a dining room is. What do I say to these kinds of criticisms? Bollocks. Usually, that kind of moaning is just sour grapes from men who can't cut the mustard. I don't agree that its inspectors are ignorant about non-French food or too old-fashioned or slow to award stars. On the first point, there are at least two Indian restaurants in London which now have stars – and very well deserved they are too. On the second, we have always found our work to be rewarded almost immediately by Michelin – you only need look at what happened to me at Aubergine to see that. More recently, Jason Atherton picked up his first Michelin star only a little over six months after *maze* opened. The Michelin Guide is nearly ninety years old now, and there is still nothing to equal its exactitude. The inspectors really do know what they are doing; they come time and time again, so it's not just about them finding you on a good day. Losing one of my stars would be like a death to me; I want to gain stars, not lose them. I want to have as many, if not more, as the great Alain Ducasse, who has fourteen and is the first chef to run three three-star restaurants simultaneously (and over two continents). When people point to our expansion and ask me if I can keep food standards high when there are so many different restaurants to worry about, Ducasse is the man I point to. If he can do it, so can I. But if I did ever lose a star, I wouldn't start pissing and moaning and saying the Guide was shit. I'd work my bollocks off to get it back, just like Alain Ducasse did in Monaco.

My third star wasn't just important in its own right: it meant that bigger, better things were around the corner. It was, if you like, an announcement of intent. Rumours started going around London that I was going to take over the kitchen at *Claridge's* hotel in Mayfair – rumours that were, in fact, not quite true. Of course, some people were sceptical. The situation was that John Williams, the Maître Chef des Cuisines there, was being moved sideways to look after room service and banqueting. But would such a smart, distinguished and historic hotel be interested in someone like me? And would I be able to put my name above the door, or would the hotel value its own identity too much to allow me to do such a thing? Most commentators envisaged a power struggle that would see me walking away from the table.

But they were wrong.

It was at this stage that we entered into an amazing relationship and one that would not only last many years, but take us into Europe and the US, and guarantee Gordon Ramsay Holdings a turnover well in excess of £1 billion in the next ten years.

We were asked to meet the General Manager of *Claridge's*, and Chris went up for a meeting. It was there in the mezzanine offices that Chris first met the amazing visionary, John Ceriale, of Blackstone Private Equity who immediately threw up the challenge by asking if I would be happy to do breakfast were we to take over the restaurant.

Chefs hate doing breakfast and Chris knew this. Clearly we were not the first to be asked this (we were probably just about the last prospects on the list) and so Chris, without missing a beat, replied in the positive. Later, he confided in me that he had wondered how to break this news to me, even saying that had it been a problem he would have done it himself. God forbid.

We were both thinking the same two things. First, that we were not going to lose out on this amazing opportunity and second, a successful breakfast operation would pay the rent, leaving the income from lunch and dinner to us.

Negotiations commenced and a deal was struck. I would be allowed to put my name above the door and, what's more, my restaurant would have its own separate entrance. In other words, we would have our own identity, but we would share the grandeur associated with *Claridge's*. I was thrilled. For me, this was a big deal. With its old-style glamour, it's a place I've always loved. Plus, its history is unbelievable.

Claridge's has been open in one form or another since 1812, and everyone has visited from Queen Victoria to Margaret Thatcher, Donatella Versace to David Beckham. It was very much a place I would like to take Tana to.

I knew, though, that people would be extra hard on me once I moved in there: the council-house boy swanking around one of London's great art-deco jewellery boxes. This made me nervous. So I was determined to get everything absolutely right. When Blackstone opened in October 2001, we had spent some £2 million on refurbishing the restaurant, reducing its capacity from 120 covers to 65. We chose an art-deco style perfectly in keeping with the rest of the hotel, a project that was undertaken by the New York-based designer, Thierry Despont, who had also been responsible for the restoration of the hotel's foyer some years earlier. The room, in shades of my favourite aubergine, is unbelievably airy and elegant; I chose all the china, glassware and cutlery myself.

I was determined to run our kitchens at *Claridge's* and the kitchen at *Royal Hospital Road* at the same time. A lot of people said it couldn't be done – that I was spreading myself too thin. All I'll say is that a lot of people wanted that gig, and they had lost out. I was lucky because I had a great right-hand man coming with me to *Claridge's*: Mark Sargeant. But I also timed the drive from Mayfair to Chelsea. It took just seven-and-a-half minutes. It seemed perfectly possible that, if necessary, I could flit between the two. I was totally fired up, so there was plenty to lose.

We spent a lot of time practising our menus. We always trial new dishes over and over until they are perfect. As a result, the menu at *Claridge's* was, and still is, exquisite. You can start with a beautiful dish like a smoked eel and celeriac soup with crushed ratte potatoes and poached quail's eggs; follow it with a roast cannon of new season's

Cornish lamb served with confit shoulder, white bean purée, baby leeks and rosemary jus; and finish with a classic caramelised tarte tatin flavoured with cardamom, and vanilla ice cream. Or, if you fancy something a little lighter, you could start off with a chilled Charentais melon soup served with a Cornish crab vinaigrette, followed by baked baby sea bass served with roasted fennel and confit garlic, and finish with blood orange semi-freddo with an Earl Grey tea sorbet and glazed pink grapefruit.

Our customers are not only men in suits on expense accounts; many of them are women, and lots of them come from out of town. I regard that as a tribute to a fantastic, well-balanced menu, and it was certainly one reason why *Claridge's* was an immediate hit. In our first week, we received over 500 telephone calls and some 300 faxes requesting reservations. In our second week of trading alone, we welcomed some 1,500 guests.

Some of the hotel's regular clients were not at all happy. One day, one of these guests accosted me in the lobby.

'Young man,' she said. 'I've been waiting for you. I've been coming here for lunch for forty-two years and now I'm told I can't have a table.'

I apologised, and asked her if she had tried to book.

'I've never had to book before, and I don't intend to start now,' she said.

She then told me how appalled she was to see the restaurant so full. What, she wondered, had happened to the days when one could have a quiet lunch with a friend without 'all this palaver'? I was lost for words.

Now we were on our way. A precedent had been set: It *was* possible to run more than one restaurant to the same high standard (the restaurant at *Claridge's* soon won a Michelin star).

My next project was to open a restaurant in Glasgow. The idea of doing so was very dear to me, for obvious reasons, though it had nothing to do with settling scores; I just liked the idea of having a success there. So we opened the seventy-seater Amaryllis inside One Devonshire Gardens, which had become Glasgow's most sought after hotel at the time. This, of course, wasn't the Glasgow I knew from my childhood: it was a different world. Glasgow was the first British city to have a Versace store outside London, and when you visit you can see why. The city is very swish, and I felt there would definitely be a market for our kind of cooking. I installed David Dempsey, and the plaudits soon rolled in. One critic described the food as being of a standard unavailable anywhere else in Scotland – and she was right. It was brilliant. Within a year, Amaryllis had won a Michelin star.

After this, we opened restaurants thick and fast. In 2002, at the request of our partners Blackstone we opened a restaurant in *The Connaught* in Mayfair. *The Connaught* is a very special place – it was named after Queen Victoria's third son – but its Grill, though a beautiful, panelled room decorated with many fine paintings, had become as stodgy as hell. It was the kind of place that made you feel like whispering. It was resting on its rather dusty laurels, serving the same old beef, and the same old Dover sole, to ageing dowagers and bufferish colonels. Nothing had changed there for years. We intended to shake things up. The old French chef, Michel Bourdain, whose haute cuisine hadn't changed one iota for years, was pensioned off, and two-thirds of the staff followed him to I know-not where.

No matter. I was going to remake the Grill Room, getting Nina Campbell to redecorate it, and installing Angela Hartnett, a brilliant cook who has been with me since my Aubergine days. She has an Italian background, and the menu was going to have a modern Italian bias – a real departure for us. I agreed that our move into the Connaught should be filmed by the BBC2 behind-the-scenes business series, *Trouble at the Top*.

This was good publicity both for the restaurant and for Angela, who could be seen working as a team with me; she dealt with me, and the cameras, admirably. The restaurant, once the wails of the dowagers had died down, was a huge success with the critics and public alike, and Angela's restaurant, Menu, went on to win a Michelin star in 2004.

After *The Connaught* experience, which was fraught with risk and difficulty, I must admit that I did feel as if anything was possible. On the other hand, I am never complacent, and when the idea of us taking on *The Savoy Grill* came up

I still couldn't quite believe it. And I thought the *Connaught* was stuffy! The Savoy is probably London's most famous hotel, patronised by everyone from royalty to Marilyn Monroe; Elizabeth Taylor spent one of her many wedding nights there.

And, more than any other restaurant in London, *The Savoy Grill* was the favoured lunching spot of the establishment. It is, famously, where Winston Churchill used to eat – after his death, his favourite table, number four, was left unused for a year as a mark of respect. On a typical weekday, you could find any number of cabinet members sitting at its banquettes, tucking into bloody meat that was delivered to them beneath a silver dome, and carved at their table. *The Savoy Grill* was very, very traditional. It still had a dessert trolley, for God's sake, heaving with trifles and jugs of buttercup yellow jersey cream. Changing it all was going to be like messing with the Holy Grail. A small part of me feared this, but another, more mischievous part thought it was a fantastic idea. After all, when the hotel first opened in 1889, its head chef was none other than Auguste Escoffier. The food at *The Savoy Grill* should be the very best.

First of all, the room had a makeover, this time by the American designer Barbara Barry. She kept the much-loved banquettes, but she infused the room with a new sense of glamour. It felt lighter, more modern and less masculine – but, crucially, it still felt like *The Savoy Grill*. In the kitchen was Marcus Wareing. By this time, May 2003, *Pétrus* had moved to *The Berkeley* where, soon after, it would be joined by our *Boxwood Café* – my upmarket take on an American diner. In other words, Marcus was going to try and pull off the same trick as me: oversee two kitchens at the same time. I knew he was more than up to the job, and so it proved. Marcus combined the best elements of the old Grill – the dessert trolley, for instance, and he continued to serve dishes like omelette Arnold Bennett – with a more modern approach. It was a triumph.

The critics loved it and so, too, did its customers – or most of them. One who didn't, famously, was my old friend, Rocco Forte. Forte was a regular at the Savoy, and declared himself appalled at the idea of change. So when he took over the old Brown's Hotel in Albemarle Street, he took Angelo Maresca, who had been restaurant manager at *The Savoy Grill* for twenty-one years, as the manager of his new restaurant – a grill, with 'daily favourites to be carved at the table'. Brown's Grill did not open for over a year and then not to good reviews. Nor does it have a Michelin star. What a shame. It breaks my heart.

Since the Savoy, we have gone from strength to strength. The *Boxwood Café*, also designed by Barbara Barry, and inspired by restaurants like New York's Gramercy Tavern and Union Square Cafe, has been a huge hit, proving those who said that I can't do anything other than haute cuisine totally wrong. I was determined that it would be a child-friendly environment and it is the only one of my restaurants where I'll allow my own kids to eat. Stuart Gillies is a brilliant chef, and the kitchen's knickerbocker glories are worth crossing London for.

More recently, we opened *maze* in Grosvenor Square. Jason Atherton, its chef, has totally revolutionised our approach to fine dining with his small portions – a flight of food with a flight of wine – a kind of upmarket version of tapas or meze. He won a Michelin star inside a year, and I would say that the *maze* bar is one of the most glamorous in London. Abroad, we opened *Verre*, at the *Dubai Hilton*, and *Cerise*, in *Tokyo's Conrad Tokyo Hotel*. Tokyo was an especially exciting challenge because my old boss Joël Robuchon was opening up there at the same time.

As I write, we have just opened our first restaurant in New York, *Gordon Ramsay at The London* and, after that we have plans to give Angela a restaurant in La Boca Ratan, Florida, and to open in Los Angeles with our great partners Blackstone. In Tokyo and Dubai, we don't own our restaurants, but we do supply the ten most important staff. Elsewhere, we own the restaurant. This is the model that works best for us, but our commitment, even when we are acting as consultants, is absolute. Make no mistake about that.

Every time I open a new restaurant abroad, the critics fill the newspapers with the same old stuff: that I am spreading myself too thin, that I am merely putting my name to projects that I cannot really control, that this expansion is vanity and money rather than the passion that was behind, say, Aubergine. It's total rubbish, of course. In the weeks building up to an opening, I am there totally: I'm hands on, putting the chefs through their paces, testing every dish, over and over. I'm too much of a control freak to do otherwise – and you see the results both in the reviews, and in the fact that our restaurants remain full long after the initial buzz is over. The other crucial point is that all my chefs are my own: they've worked for me for years – they've worked their way up, I trust them implicitly. I am not a natural delegator, but that doesn't matter one iota when you're effectively running the best training school in the business. I've got people I can rely on. People ask me who does the cooking when I'm not there, and my answer is always 'the same people who do it when I AM there'.

In any case, as the group grows, I've got a secret weapon up my sleeve. My restaurant in *Royal Hospital Road* has recently reopened following a summer-long million-pound refurbishment. The kitchen is almost like a studio – a place for an artist to work. There's upfloor lighting, and every chopping board is spotlit. It's moody and cool.

What makes me really pissed off in the kitchen? What makes me explode? Lies.

A chef can overcook a scallop, they can overcook a fillet of beef, they can overcook a turbot. But what they can't do is lie about it. That really upsets me. It's not the fact that they're lying to me; they're lying to the customers, too, and I won't have that.

If there's a cook who's completely transparent, and he looks me in the eye, and he tells me straight off: 'Yes, chef, that dish went out of the kitchen before I seasoned it', then he's got my trust. He's made a mistake, but at least he's honest. But if he lied, if he crossed that line, it would take me years to trust him again – assuming, that is, that I kept him on at all. That's the first thing we teach our chefs: not to lie. Even if it's born of panic, of a fear of getting into trouble, that doesn't change the fact that it's a great big lie. I don't want to sound too fucking gourmet about it, but you can't have chefs relying on the idea that the customer will never spot a small mistake. I won't have them ripping the customer off in that way. Also, small mistakes count. A few small mistakes equals one giant cock-up.

The second thing I can't stand is dirty cooks. I want clean trousers, clean hair and clean nails. I want a chef to take pride in his appearance. If he's proud about how he looks, he's proud about how he cooks. All of my chefs are immaculate, no matter how hot the kitchen, or how long the shift they've been working. Since we brought in the idea of the Chef's Table – a table that's right in the heart of the kitchen, where customers can see all the action – this has been more important than ever. We have a Chef's Table in all our fine-dining restaurants now, and they're usually booked for months in advance. They're amazingly popular, especially, ironically, with people who want a bit of privacy for their guests. In 2002, Tony Blair celebrated his forty-ninth birthday at the Chef's Table in *Claridge's*; it's also been used by Andrew Lloyd Webber, Richard and Judy, Ronnie Wood and Kate Moss. That one table alone generates £1m a year for our company.

Now, on paper, the idea of eating in the kitchen, among all that sweat and steam and noise, all that testosterone, sounds like a mean one. Why would anyone want to do it? But our kitchens are gleaming, tidy places, and quieter and calmer than you'd imagine. We've got superb, beautiful dishes to get out; we're not performing monkeys.

The third thing I can't stand is clock-watchers. There's no room for clock-watchers in a kitchen. You could be working twenty hours on the trot. So what? That's the way it goes.

I remember when we were at Harvey's. Sunday nights, having worked a seventy-, eighty-, ninety-hour week, we'd go to the Rock Garden in Covent Garden, see a band, have a burger. We'd leave at one or two in the morning, and we'd get a cab straight to Wandsworth, where we'd sleep on the restaurant banquettes and use a tablecloth as a sheet knowing full well that there was no way any of us was going to be late on Monday morning.

What's my idea of a clock-watcher? Someone who's more interested in the last bus than in the last table. Many times, when I was working in Paris, I'd walk home from work and still have to be the first in the kitchen, waiting for the produce to arrive, waiting to deliver the celery to the vegetable section, the beef to the meat section. The idea is the cooks arrive, and their stuff is waiting for them, like a Christmas present. I was Father Christmas. If their vegetables weren't there, they'd be pissed off. But if you'd set up their section for them and it was all ready to go, they'd be more willing to teach you. You've got to kiss arse to get somewhere, to learn. Clock-watchers are no good at kissing arse.

And there's no place for mummy's boys in a kitchen. Young chefs that involve their parents are making a massive mistake. You've got being at home until you're sixteen or seventeen, and then you've got the kitchen. The two are, and should be, entirely separate. You've got to stand on your own two feet. If you've got some good emotional support outside the kitchen, that's great. That's an advantage. But when parents are involved in their children's careers, when they start saying: 'I think my son should be cooking fish now because he's been on the staff for six months,' my attitude is: Fuck off. Look for a new job. We always encourage chefs to bring their parents into the restaurant to eat. It gives both parties a fresh insight into the work. But then I'll ask them a simple question: do you want to go out and eat with your parents? If they say 'yes', if they'd rather be choosing pudding with mummy and daddy, then I'm afraid they'll soon be looking for a new job.

But there's one thing above all that I have grown to despise and that is a fat chef. I should know, I was one myself once. That's why I started running.

It was Chris who got me into it. I was playing him at squash. It was 2000. I was 17-and-a-half stone, a real chunky monkey. He used to cane my arse on the squash court. Every time he was pissed off with me he used to take me out on to the court and completely muller me. He would take on three of us in a row, the ball crusher, me, and my two brothers-in-law Adam and Luke. He wouldn't let us out until we were on our knees. I used to be desperate to beat him, but the truth was I couldn't play squash for any longer than 15 minutes. Anyway, one day, after a match, he told me to get on the scales. I dropped my towel I was so desperate to come in as light as possible, but it was no use: there it was, my enormous weight. 'You want to do something about that,' he said. 'We're not playing squash any more, tomorrow we'll go for a run instead. In three months time, you're running in your first London marathon.' So he'd obviously planned the whole thing.

So we'd have these little meetings while we ran. I used to get quite excited. I'd run from Battersea to Mayfair to meet him, as a warm up, but he'd just berate me for wasting energy I'd need on the run – and he was right. The first marathon was awful. I was walking after seven miles. Fuck, it was bad. By the time I finished, it was dark! But that spurred me on. My first marathon I did in four hours and

ABOVE: Receiving the award for national Chef of the Year 1992, from Susan George.

BELOW: With one of my mentors, Albert Roux, at Aubergine for the launch of my first cook book, *Passion for Flavour*, in September 1996. Can't believe how young and clean-cut I look.

ABOVE: Me with Marco at Harvey's in 1989. By this time, I was his sous chef. We're dressing red mullet.

LEFT: With Marco, in friendlier times. I think this was taken at his wedding to Mati in 2000.

The staff of Aubergine, taken after we had won our first Michelin star in 1995. It's a fantastic photograph because so many of the people in it are still with me now. The two men in ties to my right are Dominic and Jean-Christophe. Dominic is now the restaurant manager at Claridges, and JC does the same job at Royal Hospital Road. To my left, you can see a young Angela Hartnett. Next to her is Mark Askew, now group executive chef at Gordon Ramsay Holdings. To his left is Freddie Foster, now executive chef in Dubai. Kneeling at the far right of the picture is a very young Neil Ferguson, who opened our restaurant in New York.

ABOVE: Me and Tana, before we were married, at the launch of *Passion for Flavour*.

LEFT: Our wedding in December 1996. We were married in a church in Little Boltons, Chelsea, and our reception, with 280 guests, was at the Café Royal.

RIGHT: The arrival of our first child, Megan, in May 1998. She arrived at a tough time, and will always be special.

BELOW: Freedom! My own place at last: outside Gordon Ramsay Royal Hospital Road in September 1998.

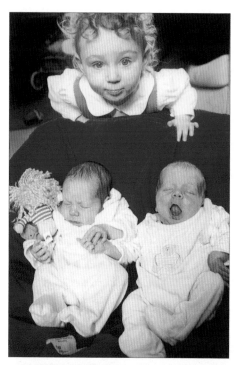

ABOVE: Megan with the twins, Jack and Holly, who were born on Millennium Eve.

BELOW: *Boiling Point*, the controversial Channel 4 series in which my temper was as hot as a flambé pan.

More arguments with Abi Titmuss in ITV's *Hell's Kitchen*. She drove me mad.

Vic Reeves approaching me at the pass during *Hell's Kitchen*. He asked for eggs on toast. 'They do them for me at The Ivy,' he said. To which I replied: 'Well, fuck off to The Ivy, then.'

58 minutes. My best time so far is 3.30 and 15 seconds, which I got in 2004. My dream is to break 3.30 and I can definitely do it. My fastest half marathon time is 1.27 – though Chris says that half marathons are for lazy men. I'm doing New York this year. I've done three Comrades in South Africa, where you run from Durban to Pieter-maritzburg.

How quickly can I tell if a new cook is going to cut the mustard? Within a day, is the honest answer – and inside a week you can identify whether they're going to be with you for two years or five. Someone who's not going to cut it is usually gone within a month. That's not to say that I don't believe in giving people an opportunity. In the early days, it was hard for young cooks to get in our kitchens. We had the Magnificent Seven – Angela Hartnett, Marcus Wareing, Mark Sargeant, Mark Askew, Stuart Gillies, Neil Ferguson, and myself – and they were working at such a pace, and to such an outstandingly high standard, that it was hard for new cooks to get a foot in the door: the bar was too high. So I used to promise people they could work those chefs' days off. I remember what it's like to work in a five-star hotel doing the banqueting, where everyone wears checked trousers and a big hat, and I know that the differ-ence between that kind of environment, which is where most people will end up training, and a real premier-league restaurant is ten miles wide. I understand that they *need* to work in kitchens like ours. It's not the kind of job where you can go out and buy an encyclopaedia and read it, absorb it, and then do it. It doesn't work like that. You need to feel it.

The easiest way for a new chef to impress me is with their seasoning. It sounds obvious doesn't it? A bit of pepper and salt. But that gives me a real indication of what a cook's palate is like. You could be the most able cook when it comes to roasting a scallop or braising a turbot, but if you can't season what you're doing, you're lost. I like to remind young chefs of how it was for me. I've still got my letter from the Mayfair Hotel, informing me that I'd got a job as second commis, grade two – whatever the hell that is – and that I would be paid £5,400 for the privilege. I can't stress enough that from a cook's point of view, the ages eighteen to twenty-eight are ten of the most important years in cooking. If, during those ten years, you haven't opted merely to take the best-paid job a job as a head chef in some second-rate hotel, say – then the chances of you surviving are high. If you've opted out and taken a job just because it'll pay you another couple of grand, or you've gone to be head chef at twenty-five because, although you've only been cooking for seven years, you like the sound of it, you're in trouble. I never employ titles, because you can't step down in this industry. You can't become a head chef and then, aged thirty, think: 'I haven't learned enough, I'm going to apply to be a commis chef with Gordon Ramsay.' I think it's the same in any job, only in this business we're ten times more ruthless. That said – I'm more patient than I was in my Aubergine days. I know I am.

My staff is mostly long-serving, which is very unusual in professional kitchens where there tends to be a very fast turnover of staff. There's a big percentage of people out there who've seen me on the TV and who think I'm an arsehole. I was once ranked alongside Chris Evans and Mohamed Al Fayed in a shitty, downmarket ITV show called *Britain's Unbearable Bosses*. That's fine; the people who come up with this crap have never worked for me, and obviously haven't bothered talking to anyone who has. I don't give a damn if some dental hygienist comes up to me and tells me that she would never tolerate my behaviour from her boss – or behave in similar fashion to someone in her employ. Kitchens are not like other workplaces. People who've worked with me, and who have survived, love it. I'm not speaking on their behalf – but ask them, and you'll see that I'm right. What they get from me is brutal honesty, and that's paramount.

Humility is important when you start out. If a young cook comes into work and he's got his name embroidered on his jacket, the first thing I'll do is grab it, and cut it out. He can spend the rest of the day walking round with one nipple on show. I've never had my name on my jacket; I still don't. When people do, it's pathetic – fucking embarrassing. They look at me like I've gone a little bit fucking loony. The name's gone – boom! – and they've got to spend the rest of the day with this big, gaping hole on their chest.

What about women in kitchens? Over the years, my attitude towards women in public has got me into a lot of trouble: I'm often regarded as the archetypal sexist git. I remember when I appeared on the BBC series, *Room 101*, with Paul Merton. I went into a huge rant about women drivers – about how rubbish they are, how unable they are to get into a small parking space, how flustered and stressed out they get. I suggested that they only be allowed to drive on Sundays. I also once said – actually I still can't quite believe that I really did say this – that women were a nightmare in the workplace, always taking time off because of morning sickness and women's trouble. 'Men talk about totty all the time in my London restaurants but women don't enjoy that kind of talk,' I said. The ensuing fuss was predictable. All the women cooks in London were immediately on my case; according to them, I was the one suffering from pre-menstrual tension.

The truth is: I often say things just to get a rise out of people. You shouldn't take every single word that I utter at face value. Angela is one of my longest-serving staff, and one of the best chefs in the country. If she makes a success of her new restaurant in Florida, I've told her that there's every chance she will go on to head up her own place in New York, one of the restaurant capitals of the world. But she's not the only woman in my employ. At *Claridge's*,

Mark Sargeant's deputy is a woman, and she's so good, there's every chance she will follow Angela and eventually open her own place, too. Overall, I must have about a dozen women working in the kitchen with me now. That may not sound like a lot, but it's a start: this has always been a male-dominated profession, and the hours don't exactly fit in with having children. But I love women chefs: they're intelligent, they're fast learners, and they can be tough. As for the effect they have on the boys, it's entirely positive. Put a woman in a kitchen and discipline will improve, if anything: the guys hate being told off in front of the girls. It's a playground thing – they just find it embarrassing.

I think my gripe with women cooks came originally from the fact that, until a few years ago, a lot of the most able female chefs in this country only wanted to be pastry chefs. On the continent, in France and especially in Italy, lots of women were heading up Michelin-starred restaurants, yet here they seemed to have no ambition. All I was saying was: stop worrying about your fondant and your Christmas cake and your spotted dick, and get in the kitchen proper and then you can be anything you want to be. I never said that women can't cook. I was just concerned that in this country, women weren't pushing for head-chef positions the way they were in France or Sardinia or Monaco. But Angela has proved that if they do have that goal, they can achieve it.

When Angela was training, we sent her off to Dal

Pescatore, a restaurant just outside Verona. Its head chef is Nadia Santini, and she has three Michelin stars. At Dal Pescatore, the women are in the kitchen, and the men are out front. After that, we sent her off to Dubai to run the kitchen at *Verre*. I told her that she was a talented cook, but that she should go out there and run not just a kitchen, but the hotel's entire food and beverage operation. She had wanted to open a basement Italian out in the East End, where she'd found a site. We were supportive, but when we looked at the lease, it was obvious that she was going to have to bust her nuts off for five years to pay back the loan and at the end of it she wouldn't have a pot to piss in. So Dubai was a kind of sabbatical for her.

'If it's a success, I swear to God as soon as I find my next site, it'll be all yours,' I said. So she went out to Dubai, and she took the whole thing totally in her stride. She can be a real ball-breaker when she puts her mind to it. After that, we gave her *The Connaught*: Blackstone saw the point of her immediately, and she got her own shares from us, a great salary package, and she's now running one of the most popular restaurants in the group. Its turnover is some £7 million a year. We're going to be right behind her when she opens in La Boca Ratan, Florida, while *The Connaught* is being refurbished. It's all starting to happen for Angela, and I couldn't be more proud or pleased for her. She's got a book coming out, and she's going to do some TV, and if all goes well in Florida, she'll be heading for New York where the kitchens are about as macho as you can possibly imagine.

The way I see it, cooking has given me the most amazing career, and a million opportunities that I wouldn't have had otherwise. Once they're on it, I want them to keep moving up it. More to the point, I need them to run the business as it grows. It's always a worry that good people will leave – or be poached – but once they are partners, once they have a stake in the business, that gets less and less likely.

So how often am I in the kitchen myself? Well, in spite of the business and all the travel, my TV commitments, the recipes I write for *The Times* and my books, and all the other millions of other demands on my time, I am still heavily drawn to my restaurants three to four nights a week at *Royal Hospital Road*, and three to four lunches.

Royal Hospital Road is the top restaurant but only has twelve tables – that's forty seats. It's closed at weekends and it's the same team for lunch, and the same team for dinner; there are no earlies, no lates, no alternate weekends. It's systematic. It's foolproof.

It's a perfect space – like eating inside a fucking Chanel handbag. In fact, it's useful to think of it in terms of fashion. A fashion house has its couture, and then it has its ready-to-wear. The couture sells the rest of the label, and all the accessories. *Royal Hospital Road* is the couture part of our business. It's bespoke food for discerning clients. That's not to say that it doesn't keep its end up financially. We turn over £3 million a year, and make between £500,000 and £750,000 a year profit – all from this tiny little restaurant. We get between 500 and 600 calls a day for a reservation – for 360 covers a week. To say that there's a waiting list for a table is something of an understatement. The waiting list for a single week alone could fill the dining room at *Claridge's* three times over. Once the list is thirty to forty tables long, we have to stop taking names altogether: it's just too embarrassing – they're never going to get in.

What makes a three-starred Michelin restaurant? Consistency. Every night must be the same performance-wise. People tend to say: 'God, Christmas must be a nightmare for you.' No, that's wrong. January is the same as December. May is the same as March. The menu is seasonal, and it changes between every ninth and twelfth week. We'll change half the dishes one week, the rest the next. Nothing must be left to chance. Because this is the jewel in our crown.

Of course, there have been failures. I'd be lying if I told you otherwise. In the early nineties, I got involved with a venture that involved Lee Chapman, the former Leeds United footballer, and his wife, Leslie Ash, the TV actress. They were moving into the restaurant business – and were setting up a dining room and private members club called

Teatro on Shaftesbury Avenue, in Soho, London. They wanted me to play an executive chef role: to draw up menus, and set the standards in the kitchen.

I asked Stuart Gillies to take charge of the kitchen, and all of the sixteen staff who went on to work with him had been tried out in one or other of my kitchens. At first, all went well. The restaurant had great reviews – the food was seriously good, so that was as it should have been – and the place was always packed: even Gordon Brown got off his spike and indulged in a night out there. But things were not great behind the scenes. As we all know, Chapman and Ash have had a difficult relationship, which has often landed them both in the tabloids. I soon decided to cut my losses and run.

I don't want to embarrass anyone, but it is obvious to anyone that knows me that, thanks to my father, I can't stand a certain kind of male aggression. Lee could be pretty aggressive. Lee used the place like it was his personal club; he was very keen to be seen shaking hands, talking to whichever celebrity was in that night. That's never been my scene – I think customers prefer their restaurateurs, as they do their chefs, to remain discreetly in the background. I didn't like the way he treated the staff. He tended to lord it, although he had almost no experience of the restaurant trade. It's not acceptable to treat people like that, and you'll never get the best out of them if you do. I'm afraid that none of the much-publicised problems that he and Leslie have had since surprised me very much. I was relieved that we got out when we did, but the experience was at least useful in that it helped us to set good working parameters when we did other consultancy projects later on.

Amaryllis, was another failure. It was a brilliant restaurant, the best in Scotland by a million miles, but I am not sure, now, that Scotland was quite ready for food cooked to that standard and at that price. Scotland is the home of the deep-fried Mars Bar, and the deep-fried Nutella-fucking-sandwich, don't forget. The restaurant was always fully booked at weekends, but during the week this was not the case. It was a special occasion restaurant, a place Glaswegians considered going to only as a huge treat, and we needed more regular business to keep our doors open. As a result, we were running at a loss; in three years of trading, we lost £480,000. In the end, we decided that we couldn't continue. No chef, however brilliant, can keep a restaurant open on just two good nights a week – it affects quality as well as the coffers because good cooks thrive on adrenalin – and so, in January 2004, Amaryllis closed. I felt extremely sad about that. I think we just misread the market.

It was a great learning curve and since then, whenever we've been planning a restaurant in a new city, we've always been extra careful to do our research, to find out what it is that people really want. In the future, I'd love to open another restaurant in Glasgow – I love the place, and I'm extremely proud of my Scottish roots. But next time, I think we'll go for something a little more informal. It's a case of horses for courses.

A more recent mistake has been our involvement with Ian Pengelley. This has taught me that the only chefs we back in the future financially must be chefs who have trained within the Gordon Ramsay Group. Pengelley, formerly of the much celebrated Notting Hill Asian-fusion restaurant E&O, was the first chef from outside the group to receive our backing and I think it is fair to say that it was pretty much a disaster from the start – a total fucking flop. We helped set him up in a restaurant in Sloane Street, Knightsbridge, on the old site of Monte's, but it lasted less than a year, and we've since broken all ties with him. There were bad reviews, a kitchen that was in total chaos and a huge gap between his idea of what the restaurant should be about, and ours. The guy used to wear flipflops to work. He was also, as he has admitted in the press, drinking. Late in 2005, we finally closed the place; we were just losing too much money to continue.

I'd be the first to admit that it was an error of judgement on our part. I was also taken in by his menu, by his fucking chilli salt squid, by all those amazing Japanese and Thai influences. It was a massive commitment on our side because, before he opened, we sent him off to Vietnam on a three-month sabbatical to do some recipe research; he went with Jason Atherton, shortly before he opened *maze*.

Ian told us all about this cookery school where you get allotted to a village in the mountains; 500 dollars buys you a stay with a family who will show you all the classic ways with Vietnamese ingredients. I was hooked by this idea because it seemed so perfect: the chefs would learn amazing new skills and recipes, and the family would earn enough dollars to buy a small piece of land at the end of it.

Maze and Pengelley's were due to open around the same time that summer. With Pengelley's I wasn't nervous; we were putting money in, but it was up to him to make a success of it. With *maze*, I was shitting myself. Jason is one of our boys, and we were trying to do something completely new. The idea was that customers ordered half a dozen small dishes, and then the staff would bring them to the table in whichever order the chef thought most agreeable.

It was like nothing we had ever done before, and I knew everyone would be watching, that all the critics would be straight through the doors, tongues hanging out, ready to slag us off if it failed – so, yes, I was really nervous.

Two hours before the doors were due to open, I had a phone call from Jason.

'I need to talk to you urgently,' he said.

'Don't tell me,' I said. 'You've got cold feet. Well, too late. We've just signed the deal, your shares have been allotted, you haven't had to put a penny in and our investment is worth a million pounds.' I was really hard on him.

Then he said it. 'I lied to you.' You already know how I feel about lies.

'What the fuck's going on?' I said.

'You know the trip to Vietnam that Ian took me on? To the cookery school? Well, it was all lies. There was no such thing.'

Basically, the two of them had just been on a jolly.

'It's been bugging me,' he said. 'I was shitting myself because I lied. But I was worried I'd lose my job.'

After Jason's confession, I put the pressure on Ian to see if he was up to it. And he wasn't, unfortunately.

Jason, I forgave. He 'fessed up, didn't he? More to the point, he's a brilliant cook, and he more than deserves his Michelin star. *Maze* got rave reviews.

Ian Pengelley, meanwhile, has disappeared into the mists of North London.

CHAPTER TEN
RONNIE

In 2003, I ARRIVED at work after the May Day Bank Holiday to find a policeman waiting for me. He wanted me to go with him to the station to identify a body – a body he believed to be that of David Dempsey who, by this time, had left Amaryllis in Scotland and was the head chef of *Royal Hospital Road*.

I was horrified at this news, sick to the bottom of my stomach, completely numb. Not only was David brilliantly talented. He was a close friend – my best friend in the kitchen world. To me, he was a kind of kid brother. We had had dinner together only the night before and, though he started the evening in quite a tense mood, by the time we went our separate ways, I had no reason to worry about him, not really – or at least, no more than usual. Now the police were telling me that he had fallen fifty feet from the window ledge of a Chelsea apartment building, having attempted to commit what would soon be reported in the press as a botched burglary. I could hardly make sense of what they were saying. But one thing was certain: there was no way I could do as the officer asked. I just couldn't face it. How could I? In the end, I asked Chris, my father-in-law to go in my place.

When the news came back that, yes, it was David's body lying there in the morgue, some of my very worst fears were realised. It soon became clear that drugs had played a part in David's death. As you are about to find out, I have good reasons for despising drugs – better reasons than most – and I will not tolerate them in my kitchens. To find out that David had been using them seemed like a terrible waste of a young life – he was just thirty-one. It seemed like a kind of betrayal. Why had he done this to himself? He had everything to live for. A loving partner and three young children. A fantastic career. It was just heart-breaking.

It's often been said in the press that, in some ways, David was a mirror image of me, and I've never disagreed with that interpretation. Like me, he had grown up in a tough part of Glasgow and, like me, his relationship with his father was difficult. His dad, who was French-Mauritanian, left home and moved away when David was just five. Like me, this history had left him with an intense need for approval, and an amazing capacity for hard work. I've never met a man who worked harder than David. His first job was in an Indian restaurant on Sauchiehall Street in

Glasgow, but on his days off he would work shifts in other kitchens, keen to have as many different experiences as possible.

This paid off. His first job outside Glasgow was at Le Manoir aux Quat' Saisons, Raymond Blanc's restaurant in Oxfordshire, and it was while he was working for Blanc that he first heard about me. He saw *Boiling Point* on television and – making rather a mockery of those so-called catering experts who insisted the show would put people off working in professional kitchens – he decided right there that my kitchen was the place he wanted to work. It was number one on his hit list, if you like.

He rang Aubergine every day until he got to speak to me personally. That impressed me. So, too, did the fact that it was seeing me on *Boiling Point* that had caught his imagination; everyone else was busy calling me a psycho and a lunatic. I told him he could do one shift at Aubergine, and that this would be his one, big chance to impress me. He accepted this offer faster than you could say crème brûlée.

His first morning, I handed him a box of leftovers. This is a favourite test of mine. I'm looking for chefs who really care about ingredients – who care as much about a few leek tops as they do about white truffles or silky foie gras, the same way I learned to care when I was in Paris. I want to see what they can do with leftovers not only because running a restaurant is about profits, about not wasting anything – but because I need to know that my staff have a feeling for food, a true love and understanding of it.

He passed this first test with flying colours. He also scored top marks in the second, when I asked him to make a simple omelette; a chef who can't turn out the basics is a busted flush. Then I found out that he was at Aubergine on his first day off having worked fourteen consecutive shifts at Le Manoir. What unbelievable commitment. I felt like he and I might be kindred spirits somewhere along the line, and I offered him a job then and there. I asked him to be a commis, which was technically a demotion in terms of what he'd been doing at Le Manoir; I supposed this was also a kind of test. I needed to know how badly he wanted to work with me. I needed to know that he was prepared to do what I had done every time I took a new job in Paris: take a step back in order to take a step forwards. He said 'yes' straight off, that was it – and within months he'd been promoted to sous chef. He was one of the strongest men in my team, and I loved him. The only thing we ever really disagreed about was football. He was a die-hard Celtic fan. I used to take the piss out of him for that, but he always gave as good as he got. He was like a little terrier.

In 2001, I asked him if he would head back to Glasgow to be head chef at Amaryllis. He didn't hesitate for a second. So we headed up to Scotland together to embark on an eating tour, checking out the competition. This is something we always do when we open a new restaurant.

You need to know what everyone else is up to, where the bar is set, what kind of stuff the locals most enjoy eating. It was David's ambition to run a Michelin-starred restaurant, and he was determined that Amaryllis would serve the best food in Scotland. I'd be lying if I said there was much competition for this accolade in the land of deep-fried Mars Bars, but still: he surpassed himself. He won that first star less than a year after the doors opened, a chip off the old block.

He was temperamental, of course. Famously, when a customer complained that his pigeon was underdone, David asked him to leave. So we always had to keep a careful eye on him. Anytime the pressure looked like it was becoming too much, we'd remind him: doucement, mate, doucement. But I thought he could handle it. I had great plans for him.

Meanwhile, things were going better and better in London and, because I was dividing my time between *Claridge's* and Chelsea, I needed a head chef at *Royal Hospital Road*. I decided that David was the man for the job, and it was great to have him there. For one thing, I knew I could rely on him. For another, he was a good person to bounce ideas off. Late at night, in the quiet after service, we would talk and talk and talk. How did he seem? Full of nervous energy, but that was always the case. I certainly had no idea that he was plagued with worries. He had money troubles, and was apparently worried that he might be suffering from a recurrence of Hodgkin's disease, from which he had suffered as a young man. On the night before he died, we went to the Fifth Floor at Harvey Nichols for dinner. The idea was that we would talk – but not about these worries, of which I knew nothing; we had a few staff issues to sort out, and it was always good to catch up. That was the last time I saw David alive.

It was only later that I found out what had happened. David had climbed up some scaffolding and had broken into an apartment building where he went round smashing windows with a golf club. No one knew why he had chosen this building – he had no connection with it. Some residents called the police. They reported that while he wasn't violent towards them, he didn't seem rational. Before the police could get to him, however, he had climbed onto a ledge outside where he tried to swing from a drainpipe on to the roof of a nearby building. That was when he missed his grip and fell to his death.

He was pronounced dead by an ambulance crew at 12.54 a.m.

I was in deep shock: we all were. The whole thing seemed bizarre and inexplicable. But right from the beginning, I feared deep down that drugs would be involved. That's certainly what the press thought. As soon as the news became public, the tabloids began crawling all over the place. One of our sommeliers was offered money for a story, any story. Reporters went rifling through our bins looking for drug-related paraphernalia. Their attitude was that David's death was an instance of me pushing my staff too far – that no one could survive a shift in my kitchen without a line of coke to get them through. I was horrified by this, for all that I feared that the truth about whatever David had taken would come out at an inquest. I will not tolerate drugs in my kitchens, and I reminded all of my staff of this in the days immediately following David's death. I knew it was important to act quickly, and I made my views all too clear in the newspapers. Our policy regarding cocaine, or any other drug, is one of zero tolerance. For a time, I even toyed with the idea of asking new staff to give us urine samples, though ultimately that proved to be impossible on legal grounds.

In the end, we found out that both alcohol and cocaine were present in David's blood on the night of his death. It seemed that David had had a highly unusual reaction to cocaine. He was suffering from a recognized delirium. As the coroner put it: 'The typical scenario is rapid onset of paranoia, followed by aggression towards objects, particularly glass.' I was called to speak at the inquest, a terrible job. I was racked with guilt that I hadn't been able to help David, that I hadn't seen any signs either of his distress or of drug abuse. If I had, I would have sent him for the right treatment, no hesitation at all. He had always stuck up for me, and I would have done the same for him.

It was difficult after David's death. I said a few things

about him in interviews that his family couldn't accept. I felt that he was still in love with Pauline, the mother of his first child, even though he was living with Fiona McClement, the mother of the other two of his children. They denied that this was true. I also said that David's mother, Eileen, was trying to find someone to blame for his death – a killer, if you like. She was understandably finding the drugs thing hard to take; at the inquest she made a point of saying that she'd never seen him take drugs. But my comments were misconstrued. It seemed like I had accused her of needing to find a murderer, and she complained to the newspapers about this, accusing me of telling downright lies, saying that of course she didn't think he'd been murdered. What I think now is that we were all in a state of grief, and a lot of things that were said should have been left unsaid.

David's sister, Yasmin, told a Scottish newspaper that she wished her brother had never met me; he might still be alive if he hadn't. All I can say is I loved David like a brother. It took me a year to delete his number from my mobile phone, where he was logged under his nickname, 'Hector'. I would never have done anything to hurt him, and I am still in touch with, and look out for, his kids to this day. I will always miss him. My world isn't the same without him.

* * *

I've said that David was a kind of younger brother to me. But his death also spoke to me about my real kid brother, Ronnie. It was a kind of warning, I suppose, a reminder of what could one day happen to Ronnie. After David died, he and my brother became inextricably linked in my mind. The one I *had* lost to drugs, and the one I *could* lose to drugs: Ronnie, you see, is a heroin addict.

He's been in and out of recovery what feels like dozens of times. I've learned not to get my hopes up where he's concerned. I've learned, I suppose, to fear the worst. David's death marks the point when this fear took on a new urgency. Before, I'd always managed to push the more harsh realities of drug use to the back of my mind. Now, I was forced to confront the fact that drugs were ruthless. They could come in and steal away the people you love most in the world at any time.

Ronnie was always in trouble, even when he was little. He was over-energetic, destructive and physically strong. He had no concentration at all. He looked more like Dad than me and, just like Dad, he was small in stature.

He was the naughty one, the one who was obviously going to follow in Dad's footsteps. I was the angelic one; he was the rottweiler. We were quite competitive with one another, because we were only eighteen months apart in age, and that was something that Dad, in his sly, sadistic way, liked to encourage. I remember one time in particular

– it must have been when we were living in Birmingham –
the girls had gone shopping with Mum, and it was just me,
Ronnie and Dad at home. I can't have been more than
eleven. Anyway, Dad made us fight. It was playfighting at
first, but it soon got out of hand. Ronnie started kickbox-
ing. I just remember trying to hide under a table, absolutely
bawling my eyes out, and him still hitting me. He was
beating the crap out of me. Of course, Dad did nothing to
stop it. He just sat there, and Ronnie got on with it.

By the time he was five or six, he was setting curtains
alight. But the trouble really started when he was about
thirteen. First, he ran away. When the police picked him up
and asked him why he was getting into trouble, he told
them it was because he hated Dad. He got a thrashing
for that when he got home. Then he started smoking,
and sniffing solvents (my deodorants, he says now), getting
in with the wrong crowd. When he and Mum and Dad
moved back to Glasgow after I had moved out to live with
Diane, he used to hang out in what were known as the
'closes' – pretty rough council estates. In these closes, there
were usually these narrow hallways and you could climb
up them, using your arms and your legs, like a spider. Of
course, most people would go so far and then give up. But
Ronnie would go the whole fucking way – thirty or forty
feet in the air – and not give a monkey's.

It was like he had no fear, no way of seeing the
consequences of his actions. There was madness in his eyes,

though I'm sure a lot of that was mostly because he felt furious at himself, furious at the way things were going. Whatever the reason, his behaviour got worse and worse. I remember once ringing home and being told that he'd been arrested for setting fire to a fairground. He spent his eighteenth birthday in Barlinnie Prison. It's category A. That broke Mum's heart.

Then – hallelujah! – he got accepted into the Team Leaders, which is a lower regiment as a preparation for joining the Army proper. Well, that was his big thing. He was going to join the Paras and his life would be sorted. I think it would have suited him down to the ground. He would have got the shit kicked out of him, learned a bit of humility. Then they would have built him back up, and that would have done wonders for his confidence. In that sense, it would have been just like starting work as a commis in a tough kitchen.

But, of course, he had to go and screw it up. He was away at camp in the Pennines, and he was caught stealing from the NAAFI. At that point he was just adding to his criminal record. From there, it was downhill all the way. He started on the heroin at twenty-one. It was inevitable. He had tried everything else, and this was just the next stage.

Then he got an HGV licence and started driving lorries on the Continent. Looking back, alarm bells should have rung then because he was always having accidents, tipping lorries over, ending up in hospital. But we were blissfully innocent. The thing about heroin is that it's one of those drugs you don't know someone is on until you see them coming down. An addict can maintain a semblance of normal life for a long time so long as they've enough money to buy the drugs they need, and that was what Ronnie did. The money he earned from driving was pretty good, and he was away for three weeks at a time, and that meant we were totally ignorant of what was going on. But then his habit got more and more serious. It was a monster he had to feed, and that was expensive. It wasn't just heroin, it was crack, too. If he did both of them together, he would get a rush from the crack, and then he'd use the heroin to level him out. By this point, of course, he was injecting, and that's when he started stealing: smash and grab a speciality. He once reversed the van into the front of a branch of Debenhams in Bournemouth so he could grab some hi-fi equipment. He could spend £2,000 a week on drugs, easy. He started running dealers round, driving them places, helping them do deals so he could get a cut. Finally, the truth came out. At this point, he stopped being Dad's blue-eyed boy. 'I knew you were a no-gooder,' he'd say. 'I knew you'd be a drug addict.' Dad just dumped all over him from a great height. He didn't give a toss about Ronnie. Whatever Ronnie says now.

He'd been an addict for seven years by the time I found out what was going on. Then it started, the endless cycle of rehab. To date, he's been through that process a number of times. The first time, it was paid for by social services. The second, I paid. Usually, he fucked it up after six weeks. In my mind, it's hard to sort the chronology of all these different visits, partly because the whole thing is such a fucking repetitive waste of time, and partly because, if I'm honest, I hate thinking about it. Seeing your little brother like that, at rock bottom, injecting the soles of his feet or his neck because he can't find a vein anywhere, or looking at his arms, which look as though someone has cut a few golf balls in half and stuck them under the skin. It's horrifying.

As for the rehab itself, I can't stand the ethos of it. I just don't buy the idea that addiction is a disease – as though a man doesn't have a choice in the matter. Usually they make you do family therapy, and that's when they accuse me of being a different kind of addict – a workaholic. I'm part of the problem, it seems. Well, bollocks to that. Addicts are selfish, the most selfish people you'll ever meet. And self-pitying. And manipulative. Always making promises they'll never keep. They disgust me. If I'm part of the problem, I'd like to know why it's me that picks up the bill every time Ronnie visits the clinic.

In the HGV days, he must have overdosed at least three times. He's done primary rehab at least three times – that's when you do the full detox – and secondary, which is when you've come out of the clinic and you're in a kind of

221

halfway house, at least four times. For Ronnie, secondary rehab was always a failure. At his lowest points, he would ring Mum and tell her that he was about to commit suicide, that he couldn't take it any more. 'I'm off,' he'd say. 'Don't come fucking looking for me. I can't go any lower now, so I'm going to take a massive big hit and that will be it.' That time, we had him sectioned, we were so afraid. He was clean for ten days, and then he was right back on the stuff, feeding a habit that was then worth in excess of a thousand pounds a week.

The things I could tell you. Once, he got some shit from a dealer in Bristol with what's known in drugs-speak as a 'lay-on'. A 'lay-on' is a kind of credit whereby you're allowed to pay for the drugs two weeks later. This particular lay-on came in at just under £1,500. The trouble was that he couldn't come up with the money. So the dealer played nice, and gave him another lay-on, only what Ronnie didn't know was that, to teach him a lesson, the guy had mixed the drugs with something seriously nasty that put him in hospital. He's never had a fixed address for longer than six months, and he's never had a bill in his own name. It's so sad and wasteful.

When David died, Ronnie was serving a three-month prison sentence for petty theft and non-payment of fines. The worst thing about that was that he never told me: it was the *Daily Mail* that kindly let me know. I won't visit him in prison. I never have, and I never will. When he's inside, I pretty much disown him. By the time he was doing this particular sentence, I was just about at the end of my tether. We had him in our house, we'd given him a job and a home, and he betrayed us over and over again, stealing from me, stealing from Tana's bag. You'd give him a tenner to go and have a haircut, and the next thing you'd know he'd be in King's Cross, buying heroin. That's always been the scariest thing about it – the sheer availability of his particular poison. I sometimes think that the only way to really clean him up would be to maroon him on some desert island miles from anywhere. I'm amazed by what his body has learned to tolerate. Amazed.

Several scenes stick in my mind. There was the time when he and I struck a deal: he could have one more score – a £10 bag – before he went into rehab. That has tortured me ever since. I had to sit and watch him. He tied the arm, waited for the vein, smacking his arm frantically because he couldn't find it, the arm swelling because it was tied so tight. Then there was this terrible moment, after the drug had hit, when he fell silent. His eyes bulged, his pupils dilated, the needle sat there. I didn't know whether to take it out, or what. I didn't know what to do. There I was in a strange house with my little drug addict brother totally out of it. I'll never forget it.

Have you ever seen heroin? I've said before that it looks like mud, like rusty water that's been left in an old bath. And then afterwards, when he told me how much better he felt, and how normal he sounded, like he was trying to prove to me that everything was okay. The gap between before and after shocked me more than watching him taking the drug itself – it showed me how easy it would be to hide an addiction, so long as you could always get your hands on the drug.

Then there was the time I went to a dealer's with him, they were these wankers with rottweilers at their feet and spyholes on their doors, immaculate in their huge shiny, new trainers. And you have to be polite, like they're some-one you really want to impress. Shaking their hands, asking them how they're doing, when all you really want is to kick seven kinds of shit out of them. The little parasites. They're scum.

But the worst time of all was the time I went to visit him knowing he was at a low ebb. I think he was living in a caravan. We went for a walk, and for some bizarre reason, we ended up in a churchyard. Ronnie broke down. I seized my chance.

'This is where you'll end up,' I said. 'You're going to be in this graveyard if you don't get your shit together.'

'But there's no way out,' he said. 'I can't come off it. I don't WANT to give it up. I want to go ... I want to follow Dad.'

This was heartbreaking.

My little brother, who'd slept on the bottom bunk bed below me for all those years, reduced to this – nothing but bones and tears. The irony of it was that when Dad died, the only way I'd been able to get him to the funeral, to carry Dad's coffin into that church, had been to watch him take a hit of heroin first. He buried my father when he was as high as a kite. Now he wanted to join him. First, he'd craved oblivion. Now he craved peace.

I'd always felt sure I would never let that happen – that, whatever he did, however badly he behaved, I would always step in and save him from himself. I saw a frail, insecure guy who had never quite recovered from being shat on from a great height by his father. I felt glad to have escaped, to have had something of my own, outside the house, that had nothing to do with Dad's music, and that only made me feel for Ronnie all the more. Now, though, I'm not so certain. At some point, self-preservation kicks in. You can't take it any more. You have to harden your heart. You have to cut the ties that bind.

After he gave up the HGV driving, I got him a job at Harvey's as a pot-washer. That was a big mistake. Our first big falling-out came one Easter weekend – the only three-day weekend any of us ever got at Harvey's. We were staying at a mate's house, and Ronnie took it upon himself to put a tab of acid into my tea. Why did he do it? Because he knew how I felt about drugs, and he wanted to wind me up. He dropped this tiny little bit of paper with a skull and crossbones on it into my cup. The worst thing was, I was about to drive the car, a fact of which he was perfectly aware. So there I was, all innocence, when all of a sudden I couldn't see straight. I'd seen the tab, but I'd no idea what it was. 'I don't know what the matter is,' I said. 'But my vision is going completely to pieces.'

I turned round, and there was Ronnie, laughing his head off. He was pissing himself. For the next twenty-four hours, I was absolutely shattered. I'd never experienced anything like it. I went to the bathroom, and I could just see my face melting away, and all I was left with was bone – it was as if what he'd shown me on the LSD paper was happening to my own face. So I went to the hospital though, of course, they couldn't do anything for me. I just had to drink plenty of water, and wait. It was extra-ordinary, as if I was walking upside down, and looking at the world upside down, and everything was just funny.

It wasn't until about two weeks later that I told him how low I thought it was for him to have done that to me. 'You know I don't smoke,' I said. 'You know that I've never taken a drug in my entire life, and then you slip a piece of paper in my tea and make out that it's part of the tea bag and then you sit there and laugh your fucking head off.' We fell out big-time and I made sure that Ronnie was booted out of Harvey's.

Years later he came to stay with us at home after

finishing his latest rehab. Tana was still a teacher at the time, working with little ones.

Living with an addict is a 24/7 business. It's a bit like having a baby. You're joined at the hip, and every five minutes you're hit with that paranoia: where is he? What's he doing? What's he up to? If he was going somewhere, we made him call us as soon as he arrived; if a journey was supposed to take ten minutes, and he took twenty, we'd be going: why are you late?

We had a big day coming up, a corporate event at Silverstone, where I was going to have the chance to drive round that famous track. I asked Ronnie to come with me. I thought he would enjoy it. But I did expect something in return: the Saturday before, Tana and I were going to go out for dinner; we needed some time alone. Ronnie had been clean for two weeks. We wanted him to behave while we were out. That's all. It shouldn't have been a big deal – it WOULDN'T have been a big deal for anyone who wasn't an addict. For Ronnie, though, and for us, it was a huge deal. We left the house nervously, with enormous trepidation, like new parents leaving a baby for the first time since its birth.

So, we got to the restaurant. He was supposed to call us, but we'd heard nothing. I wondered what was going on and so, in the hope that once I had spoken to him I would be able to relax, I tried his phone. No answer. I tried again. No answer. Tana told me to relax: we hadn't been out for a month. But, of course, it was impossible. The entire evening was ruined from the moment he failed to answer his phone. We didn't wait for our main course, we just got into the car and tried phoning again. This time he answered. I could hear a lot of ugly shouting and screaming in the background. I knew straight away the scenario that was going down. To cut a long story short, these were the sounds of King's Cross, where he'd gone to get a hit. He was using again, just two weeks on. Tana burst into tears. I felt like doing the same myself.

I went to pick him up. God alone knows how he managed to give me the right directions. When I got there, he was completely out of it. He was so far gone on the drug, like a fucking vegetable. The fact that he hadn't used for a couple of weeks had meant that the drug had a stronger effect on him than usual. He was barely conscious, slipping in and out of sleep. When he'd wake up he'd talk about our planned trip to Silverstone. 'I can't wait to go driving,' he'd say. 'You know I'm going to beat you. You're a real shit driver.' Then he'd fall back into his half-sleep again. It was awful.

But still, I gave him another chance. I took him home, and on the Monday, I took him to Silverstone with me. He was all over the shop. I remember sitting there on the M40 looking at him waking up with a jump, and coughing, the saliva dribbling out of the sides of his mouth. He was still totally out of it.

When we got back, that was when he stole from Tana. At that point, she said: 'Look, if he doesn't go, I'm going to go.' We'd just got married, we'd just bought a flat. Now she was telling me that she was prepared to go and live with her parents again.

'I can't have it,' she said. 'My drawers have been gone through, my underwear has been tipped upside down, he's even taken a pile of pound coins I'd collected up.' Tana's view was that he had been stealing from us from day one, and had managed to hide it. But now he'd got desperate, and we'd caught him.

I confronted him. Of course, he denied it. I came very close to punching him that night – a whisker away from punching his lights out – but he was under the influence of his precious drugs at the time and I just couldn't do it. That night, he went out and he didn't come back. The next morning, I went in to work at seven. It was early days for me, and money was so tight I used to do everything myself, even paying the suppliers. I wanted to be able to account for every penny I spent myself; I wasn't willing even to put it in the hands of my sous chef. Anyway, I opened the door, and there Ronnie was, completely out of it. When he came round, I drove him home. Then we got in his van – it was always a van that he drove – and we went to a garage on the Wandsworth Road to fill it up, and then I literally told him to fuck off. 'Just get out of my life,' I said. 'Get out.' All he had in the world was ten pounds. And that was it: he disappeared again. The speed with which he would come in and then out of our lives never ceased to amaze me.

In 2004, I put up cash to get him through another rehab programme, at the Clouds clinic. This time, he made me a lot of promises. Mum had been taken ill with angina, though at the time we thought it was a heart attack, and she was in hospital. When her husband, Jimmy, was told about this he had a stroke. So then they were both in hospital, Jimmy in one ward, Mum in another, both of them attached to various machines, everything being carefully monitored. It was terrible.

And then in walked this ghost – this terrible, frail-looking man who must have weighed all of seven stone. It was Ronnie, come to visit. We looked at each other and he broke down. But he couldn't stay. The last thing the hospital wanted was an addict wandering the corridors.

I hadn't seen him for close to nine months before that, and it was a terrible shock. He was drawn and gaunt; big, black marks all over his face and body, lumps everywhere. He'd been injecting in the soles of his feet and in his arse and he was an absolute fucking mess, like something out of the zombies. His cheekbones were like knives. He couldn't eat; he could barely walk. He begged me for one more chance. He told me that, this time, he really wanted to make it. Like a fool, I believed him. Why? Well, the circumstances hardly helped in terms of me being able to see clearly. Mum smoked like a chimney then, and there was Jimmy having had a stroke – two of the closest people in my life in hospital. Add Ronnie to all this, and it felt like there was every possibility that I would lose all three of them in the next twenty-four hours. The thought was unbearable. So I did it: I got on the phone, I arranged for the money to be sent to the clinic, and Ronnie was admitted exactly an hour after the money arrived at the bank. I didn't think he'd make it, but I was willing to try anything.

I feared the worst – both in terms of his health, and in terms of what he might do next. He'd reached a point where he'd actually phoned me and told me that he was going to commit an armed robbery he was so desperate for money to feed his habit. At the time, I asked him if I could call the police but, of course, the police aren't interested in you until you've actually committed a crime; talking will get you nowhere. It was so pathetic. He'd been going round factories in Taunton and Bridgwater, near where he lived, looking for pallets to chop into firewood which he then put in bags and try to sell door to door, firewood for a pound a bag. He'd persuaded the people at the Big Issue that he was a recovering addict, and they'd given him a badge, and allowed him to be one of their sellers. Except that his story was pure lies. He just screwed them for the cash, that's all. He even used to collect stray trolleys, and take them back to supermarkets so he could claim the odd pound. It was desperate beyond belief. I felt ill thinking about him in his squat, with its dingy, dreary little lights, and its damp patches, and no wallpaper, half-eaten Pot Noodles everywhere, and beds that hadn't been changed for months on end.

So, this time was supposed to be his last. 'I'm ill,' he said. 'Give me one more chance.' I asked Tana how she felt. All she could see was the terrible guilt in my eyes. This guy wasn't one of my sous chefs, he was my *brother*.

He was fucking thirty-seven years of age, he hadn't got a pot to piss in, he had a criminal record, he'd been a junkie for ten years. I needed to do something about it. So I did. I tried. I did it for him, and me, and most of all, Mum. Whatever happens now, at least I will be able to say that I tried.

Clouds clinic. I can tell you every fucking thing about the road to Clouds House in Wiltshire – every pub, every petrol station, every fucking fir tree. I would time my visits there with an open day at the Thruxton Motorsport track so that on my way back to London from the clinic, I could get out there and bust my nuts driving. I used to drive round like a lunatic, almost on the verge of killing myself, because I needed to let off steam. That was my reward, because I hated Clouds. I hated everything about it – the fact that you weren't even allowed to wear aftershave (recovering addicts are super-sensitive to smells and after-

shave has alcohol in it); the fact that you weren't allowed
to wear any kind of logo on your shirt, not Wrangler nor
Levi's nor Calvin Klein; the counsellors themselves, who
wouldn't let me see my brother until I'd told them all about
my week, who insisted I was just as much of an obnoxious
addict as Ronnie, in my way, and made me admit as
much to the rest of the group; all these strangers, hugging
you. I couldn't help it – I despised it. But I did it for
Ronnie. I bit my tongue and got on with it, and Ronnie got
clean. Again.

While he was at Clouds, out of the blue, I got a letter.
It was from a guy called John, an ex-addict himself. He'd
been sent to prison in Australia for carrying coke and then,
once he was inside, he got addicted to heroin, like so many
prisoners do. Now, he was clean. Anyway, he'd read about
Ronnie in the press and now he was suggesting himself as a
buddy: I would get him to spend twenty-four hours a day
with Ronnie, seven days a week. It was an amazing letter,
beautifully written, clever and compelling. I decided to
meet him. I should have known then that his relationship
with Ronnie was doomed to failure.

At the time, I thought he was the answer to all my
prayers. I thought because he was a recovering addict
himself, he would know best. Also, if I am honest, I was
just a little bit relieved at the idea that I would not have to
shoulder the responsibility of looking after Ronnie again,
because I knew he couldn't live with us.

I should have listened to the people at Clouds. They were dead against it.

They told me that Ronnie didn't aspire to becoming a mature recovering addict; he was in a much more juvenile state. When he was in Clouds, he fell in love with a girl, which is strictly forbidden; addicts are not allowed to have relationships with one another. Then, when he came out, he had a beer. Technically, that beer signified a relapse. I've got friends and customers who are clean – and that means CLEAN. Nothing. They're allowed nothing. Not even a glass of Buck's fizz.

We introduced John to Ronnie about three weeks before his six-week rehab was due to finish, and when he came out, he went off to Ireland to stay with him for a while. The plan was that Ronnie would go out to Thailand as a volunteer, to help with the rebuilding work after the tsunami. This was John's brilliant idea and, looking back, perhaps it was pretty naïve of us to go along with it. Thailand is not exactly what you might call a safe haven for the average recovering addict. But John was going to be with him. I was totally reassured by that. I liked the idea that they would be doing some good in the world. I thought seeing people who had suffered so much would give Ronnie a sense of mission, a sense of purpose.

Unfortunately, however, they soon started taking the piss. The rebuilding work went on the back burner, and they started living the high life instead. It was clear that he had surrounded himself with idiots and spongers, that he was playing the big dick again. At one point, Ronnie rang me and told me that he needed a holiday.

'Say that again,' I said.

'I need a holiday,' he said. 'It's so depressing here.' So much for the suffering of others giving him a bit of perspective. He then promptly disappeared into the mountains for ten days.

One night, the pair of them went out and got absolutely paralytic. Another time, Ronnie got a motorbike, took some girl for a ride on it, and crashed. Neither of them was wearing a helmet. Well, that really set the alarm bells ringing. The Thai hospital was a nightmare. He had a huge hole in his foot. He would ring up Mum in England to tell her what a terrible state he was in. 'Have you any idea how much pain I'm in?'

He'd scream down the line. 'I can't get out of this fucking hospital.' And no sooner had he been discharged than he stood on some kind of poisonous shell on the beach and he was straight back in again. Project Thailand seemed to be going well and truly tits up. At that point, we brought Ronnie home. Chris picked up him at the airport, and before he had even had time for a cup of tea, took him straight to the hospital to be tested. I needed to know that he was still clean. I think I can be forgiven for having had my doubts.

Luckily for him, the tests came back clear. So off he

went, to Thailand. By this time, he and John had fallen out. He was on his own. I can't say I felt optimistic about what would happen next.

Before he left for Thailand I bought him a new set of teeth to the tune of £28,000 (his teeth, like those of all addicts, were well and truly fucked; he said the only way he could get his confidence back, so he could work again and talk to girls, would be if he had a new set). But was he grateful? Of course not. He wasn't even proud of the new teeth; he's smoking again, even though he promised he wouldn't.

By December 2005, I had finally had enough of receiving no news or progress report and I told him that his time was up, that he had to come back. But before he left he was on the telephone to me telling me that he couldn't leave Thailand until I'd sent £150 for his hotel bill. The hotel wouldn't give him his passport back until he paid them. The money he owed was all for room service, 'what room service?' I asked.

'I have to eat and drink,' he said.

'Why can't you just do a fucking day's work?'

But he always has an excuse. This time, it was the tsunami. That really stuck in my throat. 'There are no jobs,' he said. 'Everyone's still recovering from the tsunami.'

When he finally did arrive in the country, he had nothing – not a toothbrush, not a can of deodorant, and certainly no Christmas presents for my kids or Mum. The only thing he brought with him was a black bin liner full of dirty washing. I was disgusted by that – the lack of effort, the lack of care on his part. But, far worse, he didn't come back looking brown and fit, able to scuba dive or run a marathon. He came back looking worse than he did before he went into Clouds. I might have been able to deal with the fact that during seventeen months – we soon found out he'd done no real work out there at all – if he had used the time to get healthy and strong. But no, he looked like a wreck.

After Christmas, I put him to work driving a van for me, doing all my handiwork, plastering and painting. After ten days, he phoned in sick. We were giving him £25 a day, and we'd set him up in a hotel in Victoria, bought him some new clothes, and he phoned in sick. After that, he disappeared. I didn't see him. He didn't phone – and he certainly didn't write. Where Ronnie used to be there was just a void, a blank. From what I can gather, he went to live by the coast again, in a caravan, and worked delivering skips. But as far as I was concerned, he was back on the cycle again; I recognized the pattern. Was he using? I felt very afraid that he was – or that he would soon. After all, he headed straight for Bristol, one of the heroin capitals of Britain. He knew where to score.

The disappointment this time was worse than anything I've ever experienced.

When he got clean, we were so happy. My Mum told me that, for her, it was like winning the lottery. She and

Jimmy have always had the worst of Ronnie, and that used to break my heart. Once, in Bridgwater, she was out shopping when she walked past him lying in a shop front. Another time, Ronnie broke into her house and stole all Jimmy's equipment (he used to be a paint blaster). Once he went to see my sister Diane's new baby, and stole her rent money at the same time. But now I felt I'd been taken for the ultimate ride. He told me he would kill himself if he didn't get into Clouds, so I made that happen – and this is how he repaid me. If it turned out that he was using again, I was going to cut him completely out of my life, for my sake and that of Tana and my kids. I swore to God that I would never ever fucking fund him again.

In February 2006, Mum became seriously ill and was taken into hospital for a quadruple heart by-pass operation. Within twenty-four hours of her surgery, when she was still in intensive care, in walked Ronnie, looking for money. He's that fucking callous. I could have killed him for that – luckily I was stuck in the US at the time, and all I knew about what was happening was hearing Mum's whispery, frail voice down the telephone line. That's how sudden the whole thing was. He was chasing a £300 payment from the DSS, and he had some idea that it had been paid into a bank account of Mum's. To me, doing that to Mum is on the same level as some of the things that Dad used to do to her. To walk in there and ask someone who might have been on her deathbed, who's recovering from open heart surgery, for 300 quid – well, you have to be the biggest fucking prick in Britain to do that.

Ronnie is thirty-nine years old and he's never had his own flat, he's never thrown a dinner party, he's never had a two-week package holiday in Spain. He's never done anything normal. I despair of him. But it's worse than that. Now, for the first time, I've been focusing on what it would be like to lose him. It's a horrible thing to say, but I've got to prepare myself. I'm getting stronger, I'm building a barricade. I don't want him in my life any more. I don't want him invading my head, I don't want my kids knowing what he is or isn't and I don't want Mum's stomach ulcers getting any bigger through worry. I know what's going to happen if he starts using heavily again, but this time, I won't open the door. I can't do that to Tana again, or to Chris, who gave me so much help last time around. I don't feel fucked or shafted, I just feel deeply, deeply hurt. It's like he's not even my brother any more.

Last year, Ronnie threatened to go to the newspapers, to tell them 'the truth' about me. He's done that before and taken money from the tabloids. A guy from the *Mirror* once offered him cash as he left one of his many court cases. He took the money to feed his habit, and I wonder if the tabloids ever considered that possibility. In the interview that he did, he didn't really have a good word to say about anybody. His line was: the world owes me something. It's all so unfair so far as Ronnie is concerned. My success is a massive part of his instability, I can see that. I didn't need a few smart-aleck drug counsellors to help me sort that one out. Well, fine.

Make a success of your own life, then, Ronnie. But of course, he won't.

Anyway, if he wants to tell the newspapers the truth, he's more than welcome. I don't give a fuck. The truth is that I've done everything that I can to help him, and none of it has worked. Unlike my dear friend David, Ronnie is still alive. But that doesn't mean that he's not lost to me because, though it hurts like hell to put this thought down on the page, I'm desperately afraid that he is.

With Tana, who was pregnant with Matilda, and my mum at the launch
of Claridges in 2001.

RIGHT: The London
Marathon 2002.
Get in, my son!

BELOW: With HRH Prince
William at Sport Relief 2004.

LEFT: Momma Cherri, owner of an American soul food restaurant in Brighton, one of the places I visited in the first series of *Kitchen Nightmares*. We really did the trick with Momma Cherri because her business is now so successful, she's just opened her second place.

American Soul Food Restaurant

RIGHT: Posing with Gillian McKeith and Jimmy Carr after accepting my BAFTA for *Kitchen Nightmares* in 2005. I was thrilled.

RIGHT: In Los Angeles, for the launch of the US *Hell's Kitchen* in 2005.

BELOW: With my Muppet Brigade – better known as the contestants in the first series of the US *Hell's Kitchen*. In the US, contestants weren't celebrities, but members of the public who wanted to make it as chefs – an idea that made for much better television.

ABOVE: With the Norfolk Bronze turkeys that we kept in our back garden for the first series of *The F Word*: Anthony, Delia, Gary, Jamie and Nigella were all named after well known cooks, and all, I'm afraid, met a hot basted end.

ABOVE: With Sir Cliff Richard on *The F Word*. We did a blind tasting of several wines, one of which was his own label, made from the grapes grown at his home in Portugal. He said they were all awful, and refused to pay for any of them. He was pretty mad and embarrassed about this afterwards.

RIGHT: FA Cup Sport Relief 25th Feb 2003.

LEFT: *Soccer Aid*, May 2006. The final, at Old Trafford, before a crowd of 75,000. Robbie Williams was the captain of England, I was captain of the Rest of The World.

BELOW: I managed to play the first half of the final. This is me arguing the toss with the ref, Pierluigi Collina. I'm saying: 'I'm inside the box! It's a penalty!' He told me not to speak to him as if he was one of my waiters.

ABOVE: With my OBE. A great day.

BELOW: The family. Our little surprise, Matilda, is on Tana's knee.

CHAPTER ELEVEN

DOWN AMONG
THE WOMEN

WHAT ABOUT THE women in my life?

Obviously, Mum has been unbelievably supportive through everything, and it's the biggest relief that she is recovered from her heart operation now and is looking so much better. She's even given up the cigarettes at long last.

And there's my two sisters, Diane and Yvonne. I'm closest to Diane because whenever the family got broken up, we two would end up together, and the younger two would end up together. Like Ronnie and I, our childhood affected them both, albeit in different ways. Yvonne was always being told to shut up, always being picked on. I suppose it was because she was the youngest. Diane was very much into music, just like Dad. I recall some photographs of them together from those days, and they look like Ike and Tina Turner. Diane would often go on the road with him, and there's no two ways about it: she did have a fantastic voice.

When Diane was fifteen Dad began to really lose the plot with her. He was becoming jealous of the fact that she was growing up, becoming an individual. Like any fifteen-year-old, her mates were more important to her than her parents. She started to rebel and didn't want to perform with him any more. The punk era came in, and she started wearing her hair all spiky. She also started smoking. If we were going out, she used to make me put her cigarettes down my pants because she knew I wouldn't get searched – my parents would never believe that I smoked. Even so, I used to sit there, trembling, white with fear, with all these Benson & Hedges, JPS and Number Six rolled up in tissue paper in my pants.

Diane had a boyfriend who had a car that just happened to be smarter and more expensive than Dad's. He didn't like that at all. He started to get really jealous. He wanted her out. He spent most of the time trying to convince Mum that Diane was such a difficult teenager that she needed to be sent away. He was losing control, and this was his solution. Unfortunately for all of us, it worked. He issued an ultimatum: it's her who goes, or me. And that was that. Diane went to live with foster parents, on a farm.

It was hugely distressing for us all, especially Mum. She still gets upset about it now, if you ask her. We'd be having our tea – ham, eggs and chips, or fish fingers, chips and beans – and there'd just be the three children around the table. Someone was missing, and it hurt. Dad, of course, was really pleased with himself, really smug.

He took advantage of Mum's vulnerability. I remember her breaking down once, and saying: 'All I want for my birthday is my daughter back.' I missed Diane, but her absence also meant that I was now the eldest; I felt as if there was a lot more responsibility on my shoulders.

Diane lived at the farm for quite a while. She was turning into a beautiful and independent young woman and that really irked Dad as he had finally lost all control.

As soon as she was sixteen, she managed to get her own council flat. That was a huge relief, as much for me as for her, and that was where I lived once Mum and Dad moved back to Scotland. Di, then, became like a mother figure to me. We really bonded.

It was around that time, when Mum and Dad were living in Dennistoun, a pretty rough part of Glasgow, that Dad starting picking on Yvonne. With Di and I out of the picture, and Ronnie increasingly in his own sorts of trouble, getting picked up by the police practically every day, the spotlight fell on her. She was just fifteen years old.

I wanted her to come live with me and Diane, but Dad would never have allowed it. Things improved for her a bit when the whole family moved down to Bridgwater. Shortly after that she fell pregnant and got her own place. Perhaps that was her best means of escape.

*   *   *

And now I've got three daughters of my own, Megan, Holly, whose twin is Jack, and Matilda. What's my attitude to these girls? Well, I certainly want them to have an easier time of it than their aunts did. But, given my own child-hood, it would be all too easy for our children to be spoilt. That's the big danger. But Tana had an amazing child-hood and she still has fantastic manners. So she's a good example. She's also a great support, not undermining me when I'm tough on them – though it wasn't until quite recently that she has understood just how difficult my own childhood was. But still, we guard against their becoming spoilt. At Christmas time, they get one present each. We don't want them sitting there, ripping open one present after another, and not appreciating anything. I want them to understand and value what they have. I really struggle with the kids sometimes: I see Jack growing up with all the things that, as a boy, I could only dream of owning, and that can be difficult. I see his Action Man, his camouflage tops and his initials being stitched on to his jumpers for school. I work hard at making sure that there's no jealousy there. But I also push him. If he goes out to play in the winter, and complains of being cold, I won't let him wimp out and come back in straight away. I expect him to tough it out. And Jack regards me as his best mate, which is wonderful because I never had that with my father. I feel that Jack was born for a reason. He wasn't due until the February, but he was early – he arrived on the millennium

New Year's Eve, exactly one year after my father had died. They all help me through life in that way, though I can't help but compare them with how we were at the same ages. The girls to Diane and Yvonne, and Jack to Ronnie. I try to imagine what it would be like if Holly took an overdose, or Megan was taken into care, or Jack started messing about with drugs. That would be fucking mad. Unbearable.

The other thing I do is always make it clear that life is about hard work. On Saturday nights, they'll say: 'Where are you going, Daddy?' I'll always be sure to tell them that I'm going to work because nothing comes for free – not their shoes, their toys, or even the milk in the fridge. They only get a pound per week of pocket money each. If they get more, it'll have been because they helped in the garden. And every summer, Mum will take them to Butlin's, so they know what a normal holiday is like, with Redcoats and buckets and spades. I'm not interested in them getting hooked on luxury. I want them to keep it real.

For the same reasons, the only one of my restaurants that they're generally allowed to eat in is *Boxwood Café*, which is family-friendly. Otherwise, they can go for a pizza, like any other kid. The only time they come to any of the other restaurants is on Christmas Day, when I'm cooking at *Claridge's*. They get a sandwich, which they eat at the Chef's Table. Out of respect for my staff, I'm not going to ask any-one to start cooking something for an eight-year-old girl.

When they're naughty – especially if they won't share

things – their toys tend to get taken down to the local refuge. And none of them will be going off to boarding school. I want them to be nice, normal kids.

Most of all, I want them to have choices in life. I swear I'll never be like our dad, who was always telling us 'I told you so' if our plans went wrong. I want them to decide what it is that they really want to do, and go for it.

Is my fame difficult for them? They're just starting to become really aware of it. I want to protect them, but I don't want to wrap them up in cotton wool. I only do one school run a term, because it does tend to mean that there will be a certain amount of obstruction outside the school gates once people get wind of the fact that I am there. But who am I kidding? I can't stand all that school stuff, irrespective of whether people recognize my face or not. I got into a lot of trouble not so long ago when I said in a glossy magazine that in my kids' school playground, I'd never seen so many pigs' trotters in my life. I meant some of the mothers – all dolled up to the nines. Those women, looked bored to tears, using hubby's little bit of plastic, trotting off to buy their lamb shanks, then a little bit of Pilates, then pick up the kids. Outside the school gates, it's a nightmare. I don't want to talk about their split-fucking-hollandaise sauce. I want them to leave me alone. So that's why I do one school run a term, and only one, no matter how much Megan likes it when I show up. Those mothers can be so fucking superficial. It's about a million miles away from the way things were at Stratford High. The nativity play is like hell on earth. All the dads rushing in with their bald heads and their pin-stripe suits, bawling their eyes out when they see their little darlings up there on stage, and the mothers rushing to the front so they can use the zoom lenses on their video cameras. Dear God. Save me from all that.

Our first three kids are the result of IVF; Matilda, our youngest child, was an accident. We'd been trying for two years before we embarked on the IVF. Tana had suffered from polycystic ovary syndrome, which can have an effect on fertility, and I had a low sperm count, the result of my balls being in front of all those hot ovens. That's a common problem for chefs, who endure all that heat seven days a week. The industry needs to develop some clever cool aprons to keep all those bollocks chilled during service. Seriously.

Knowing why I had a low sperm count means I've never felt inadequate about it. Though I felt badly for Tana when she couldn't get pregnant. It was especially hard for her at the time because she was teaching small children. But that kind of thing either puts undue pressure on your relationship, or it brings you closer. It brought us closer. Still, it wasn't easy. We went to hell and back. I had to masturbate into a little bottle and do my tadpole thing. Afterwards, they said: 'The bad news is your sperm count is low. The good news is that the ones you do have are very energetic.'

We'd found out we'd been successful, that the IVF had worked, on the same day that Diana, Princess of Wales, died. We were feeling pretty quiet and saddened, and were expecting the worst in the early hours of that Sunday morning. We were on our third try by then. But, it was good news – for us, at least. Later, with the twins, we were successful the first time.

Megan, our eldest, will always be special, because every birthday that she celebrates, I remember Aubergine and how tough things were, how hard I was working. By the time the twins came along, we were more secure, though not much more – we were still living in rented accommodation. I was shitting myself. Then again, there's never a right time, especially in my industry, and I guess the knowledge that I had all these mouths to feed just spurred me on. We didn't expect to jump from one to three, but that seems to happen a lot with IVF.

With Matilda, well, I thought Tana must have gone a bit bonkers. She had come to the restaurant kitchen to tell me the result of the pregnancy test she'd done unbeknown to me.

'Tana,' I said. 'I'm up to my eyeballs in shit. What is it? Have you crashed the car?'

'No, no. Look on the table ... Look at the stick ... I'm pregnant.' And she burst into tears.

I've never been present at the births of any of my children

and, as just about everyone in Britain now knows, neither have I ever changed a nappy. I've taken a lot of shit over the years for both these things. I was labelled the ultimate sexist git, chauvinist pig, a total arsehole. I got completely panned by just about every woman journalist going. But look, let's be honest. Changing nappies is not exactly the most appetising task in the world. As for the birth, what people seem to forget is that Tana had a say in the arrangement as well. Giving birth is a very fraught kind of a scenario. Being such a control freak, I'd be the last person anyone would want in there. Tana wanted her mum with her, so I would just slope off to Syon Park and do some fly fishing while I waited for the call. When Megan was born, it was my father-in-law's birthday, and I went down to The Ivy to celebrate with him. I needed time to prepare myself. I was incredibly nervous about seeing the baby.

I arrived at the hospital absolutely pissed. 'Are you sure it's a girl?' I said, and pulled the blanket off her just to check. For some reason, I'd been absolutely convinced we were going to have a boy.

I couldn't have handled being at the births, and I don't mind admitting it. Emergency situations, I can handle. But not gore. Not placentas. I'm useless at it, absolutely fucking useless. I imagine childbirth as like being stuck in a room with a thousand skinned rabbits. When Tana turned round and told me that she didn't want me there, I was fucking relieved. I had this image of an alien in my head.

But I don't think my kids love me any the less because I wasn't there. We've still bonded. Sometimes, I walk down the King's Road and I see guys with babies on their chests, and babies on their backs, and the woman is walking alongside concentrating on her shopping. It won't surprise you to hear that that's not me at all. I loved them as babies, but I like it much better now I can actually communicate with them.

In any case, all seems to be forgiven now. The other month, I won an award for Father of the Year. It was from *Glamour* magazine, I think.

How the tables have turned. Personally, I'd like one more child. Another boy, maybe, so that it's not just me and Jack versus all those women. But Tana's back in her jeans now, so I'm pretty sure I can whistle as far as that dream goes.

In the end, of course, we moved out of Stockwell and rented accommodation – to Wandsworth, and a massive place that used to be divided into flats. It's a wonderful house, and one that has become famous in its own right. Thanks to my Channel 4 show, *The F Word*, we've kept turkeys in the back garden, as well as pigs. Tana was horrified; on both occasions, she couldn't wait for them to go. But the thing that really seems to have caught people's attention is the kitchen. Well, the two kitchens, actually.

Lots of couples have 'his and hers' washbasins, or 'his and hers' bathrooms. Not us: we have what the press likes to call 'his and hers' kitchens. Tana's is on the lower ground floor. I once described it in print as an 'MFI' job, which is a bit of an exaggeration and probably pissed Tana off no end, but you get the picture. It's your standard fitted-kitchen, and it's where Tana cooks the kids' meals – or Mum, if she's staying. It also used to be where Tana would keep some of her more outrageous supermarket purchases – ready meals, stuff with Jamie Oliver's name on it, that kind of thing – though she's given up all that now. It used to wind me up no end. These days, she's a great cook – good enough to be publishing her own recipe collection, in fact.

My kitchen is on the ground floor. It's where we do all of the shoots for our website, and for the weekly column that I write in *The Times*. It cost some £500,000 to put in, and includes a main oven the size of a car (yours for £67,000) and two dishwashers. The door handles are based on Ferrari gear sticks, and the extractor fan is totally silent, and so powerful it makes Megan's hair stand on end if we stick her beneath it. This is totally my domain though I'm a lot less possessive about it than the press makes out. For one thing, Tana is the only one who knows how to use some of the gadgets, the coffee machine included. If she's out, everyone has to make do with tea. For another, my chefs are usually all over it, trying out recipes, setting stuff up for photographic sessions. In any case, let's face it, I'm hardly ever home for long. Do we do dinner parties? Yes. But you won't find me faffing about in the kitchen whipping up a soufflé. At home, Tana cooks downstairs in the MFI kitchen, or we get takeaway, or we grill something simple. I want to be able to enjoy myself. I'm not interested in a busman's holiday. This isn't because cooking isn't my life. It is. It's more that I'm such a perfectionist that it really wouldn't be much fun for my guests if I was in the kitchen. I don't like distractions when I'm cooking. I need to focus. And in my experience, my kind of focus doesn't mix too well with small talk and nibbles . . .

CHAPTER TWELVE

WELCOME TO THE SMALL SCREEN

THE FIRST BIT of television that I did after *Boiling Point* was a programme for the series *Faking It*, which was shown on Channel 4. This show restored my faith in TV – though first signs, I must admit, were not auspicious. The idea was that I would train Ed Devlin, who had his own burger van in the North of England, to be a top chef. He was going to come and work with me in the kitchen at *Royal Hospital Road*, at the end of which he would be ready to compete against some real top chefs in a competition. I had just four weeks in which to pull off this minor miracle.

The first day, this dirty little fucker with roll-ups and yellow teeth walks in. He had on this stupid cap, the kind of thing the rag-and-bone man used to wear when I was a kid – a woolly, flat cap. And he had an unbelievably strong Geordie accent. It was clear that the producers of the show had been quite successful at avoiding giving me too much information before the start date.

Had I known that this specimen would be invading my kitchen, I think I would certainly have passed on giving him his fifteen minutes of fame. When I put him to work, things got even worse: it was obvious that he hadn't a clue about food – no feel, no touch, no palate. Dear God.

There was no love lost between us from the outset. He came in with lots of attitude, lots of big ideas about himself, and about kitchens. He kept saying things like: 'These little strips are julienne, aren't they?' To which I would reply: 'Fuck the French. They're little strips to you, okay? Fuck the julienne, just cut me some little strips.'

Then he'd go off into a little sulk. He was always working against me. My response to that was to give him a harder time. I knew that I didn't have long, and I needed to pull down the barriers that he had put up.

The trouble was that this was the early days of *Royal Hospital Road*, long before we opened in *Claridge's*. I couldn't allow anyone to fuck up my restaurant. But there he was, bursting into laughter in the middle of service. One night, I took him outside for a little word. I told him that we didn't tend to shout and laugh in the kitchen. Our work was far too serious for that.

'Well that's just fucking ridiculous,' he said. 'You've got to have a laugh.'

'Yeah, but not between seven o'clock and eleven o'clock, you don't. Once we finish cooking, I don't care what you do. But don't let me catch you laughing in the middle of service again.'

The next day the little fucker didn't come back.

The producer asked me if there was any way I could be a little easier on him. I was amazed. 'What do you mean, a little easier? He's got to get up to speed. I'm trying to turn him into a serious chef, but he's a tough nut to crack.' I lost it a bit, then. 'Look, I'm really happy to work on this, but you're not going to screw my restaurant for one little fucking Geordie who wants to smoke fucking little Old Holborn rollers every two minutes.' I did an impression of him, the way he held his cigarette between two fingers, his face all pinched and tight, the sucking noises he used to make when he took a drag.

Finally, we had a massive run-in. I took him outside again.

'What the fuck are you doing this for if you're not prepared to try?' I asked.

'No one's ever told me what to do before,' he said.

'Well, let me tell you this. You've got a chance to do something big here.'

And then he broke down, and it all came out. How he'd had a drink problem, how he'd been through rehab. We sat together for three hours on the kerb, and I told him all about my problems with Ronnie and Dad, and then we went and had something to eat together, and all of a sudden, that was it. Commitment, at last! The next day in the kitchen, his head was down, I barely knew he was there. He was so focused.

For the show's big set-piece climax, he had to cook dinner for a set of judges alongside a group of other young chefs, some of whom had been in training for ten years or so. The judges had to decide which of these young men would make a head chef, and try to spot the fake. Well, fuck me if my little fucker didn't win it. He didn't just garner praise from the judges: he won it. I felt so proud of him. There was a moment when the judges were coming round the kitchen, talking to each of the contestants in turn. When they reached Ed, I heard him say: 'Would you mind just giving me two seconds while I just finish cooking this red mullet.' It was amazing – the way he put his hand up and practically told the judges to shut up because he was at a critical stage. I think that move alone may have won it for him; in their minds this guy couldn't possibly be a fake. I would have loved it if Ed had gone on to become a chef. He proved he had the talent. Unfortunately, that wasn't to be. Still, the programme went on to be sold to the US, and all of a sudden I was getting interest from the people in TV.

After a few false starts – I had been in discussions with the BBC to do a kind of culinary boot camp, taking youngsters and turning them into chefs, only it was turned down on the grounds that it was too 'heavy' – I met Pat Llewellyn, who runs Optomen, the production company that makes my Channel 4 shows. *Kitchen Nightmares* was inspired by a series that Optomen had also made for Channel 4 called *If You Can't Stand the Heat*, in which a guy called Pat McDonald visited failing restaurants, giving them advice. I knew McDonald from my Harvey's days. I recall him turning up at Harvey's to show Marco a samurai warrior carved out of lard. What a complete wombat. Anyway, the show was a flop and sank without trace. But one of the producers at Optomen said to Pat Llewellyn, look, let's remake it, but modernise it a bit, because the idea has still got legs. So that's what they did. Only this time, the troubleshooter was not Pat McDonald, but me.

The series has been an amazing success – and, I think, a real eye-opener for those people who misguidedly believe that a food revolution has taken place here in Britain, and that we are now blessed with fantastic eateries in towns up and down the land. I don't think so. The places we visit for *Kitchen Nightmares* are genuinely awful: dirty kitchens, with chefs who use packet sauces, dining rooms like something out of the *Mary Celeste*. We've seen it all, and everything we screen is absolutely as we find it, I can promise you that. We recently accepted £75,000 libel damages against the London *Evening Standard*, whose TV critic, Victor Lewis-Smith, had alleged in one of his reviews that an episode of *Kitchen Nightmares* that was filmed at a restaurant called Bonaparte's in West Yorkshire was rigged, that me and Optomen were guilty of 'gastronomic mendacity' – that we had installed an incompetent chef and fabricated culinary disasters. This was complete rubbish, which was why we won – the restaurant *was* a total disaster. As I said after the case was over, we've never done anything in a cynical, fake way. There's no need. You couldn't make most of these places up.

The working title for the show was *Ramsay's Restaurant Rescue*. Then I came out of the very first restaurant we visited . . .

'This is a fucking nightmare,' I said to Pat, no doubt with genuine terror in my eyes.

'That's it!' she said. 'We'll call the show *Kitchen Nightmares*.' She had an excited gleam in her eye.

'Fuck the title,' I said. 'I don't think you're listening. It's like a horror film in there.'

People think stuff is set up. No way. The production staff doesn't even give me any background before I get there so my reactions are all completely genuine. I never meet the restaurateurs in advance, nor do I get to read their menus. If I did, half the time I probably wouldn't bother showing up. The bottom line is, the secret of the show lies in its rawness, in its rough edges.

I have a whirlwind eight or nine days at each restaurant to turn things round. We barely sleep while we're filming. We film between seventy and eighty hours of footage to make each forty-eight-minute show. The difficulty for the restaurants is after I've gone. When their restaurants aren't full they start to panic. But you can't turn a business round in eight days. What you can do, however, is implement some key changes – work on the basics – so that when we come back for another visit two or three months later, they should be up there, making a go of it. One thing I always do is to make sure that, after I've disappeared, friends, family and production staff go and eat there – even restaurant critics. I'd say that 75 percent of the time, we leave on a positive note, with the business in better shape and the staff a good deal more positive and happy.

In a funny way, the most satisfying programmes for me are not the ones where we find mouldy béchamel sauce in the refrigerator, but the ones where the chef can cook and knows about ingredients, but is somehow lost. I remember filming a show with a guy who used to have a Michelin star; now he's running a restaurant in King's Lynn. Halfway through filming, he threw me out, and the only way I could get back in was by waiting outside until lunchtime service began, and then going back in as a customer.

His produce was all high end. Even his fucking sausages came from Toulouse. Best ends of lamb, French pigeon, cheeses from France. Expensive stuff. The guy had all my books, and some of my recipes on the menu. Basically, he thought he was me, but he was living in KING'S LYNN. I had to remind him of where it was that he was trying to make a living.

'How do you decide on a menu?' I said.

'I look at my cook books,' came back the reply.

Wrong. Your location decides a menu. The guy wasn't even quite sure of how much he needed to take a week to survive. He had the frills and all the trimmings, but his business was losing money. It was all about his ego, about the stupid diamonds of chicory he would do to accompany a cheese soufflé. Ridiculous. He was obsessed with baby vegetables. But why spend £3.50 on a bag of carrots from Kenya, when you can get them locally for 90p. There's no doubt that he could cook, but he wasn't interested in the graft; he just wanted to put his paintbrush over everything at the end and sign it.

There are lots of chefs like this in Britain just now – chefs who are waiting for medals and acclaim, but don't give enough attention to anything to do with the customer. But it's really all about the customer. No one should ever forget that, no matter how great their sauces are.

And so to *Hell's Kitchen*, one of the worst experiences of my life. Originally, the idea was that there would be two teams in competition with one another, the other of which would be led by Anthony Bourdain, the bad-boy New York chef and author of *Kitchen Confidential*. Originally, it was going to be on Channel 4, but that plan went belly up and it ended up going out on ITV. Channel 4 brought forward the transmission of *Kitchen Nightmares* to precede it, so it was a mad few weeks.

I honestly had no idea of how big the show was going to be – the scale of the kitchen that they'd built, the size of the restaurant. Meanwhile, Chris was going: no, no, no, NO. He was hugely against the idea, on the grounds that it was basically a reality TV show.

But I was naïve. The challenge appealed to me – the idea of having all these novice cooks in the kitchen, and of running the whole thing live. Then, when I persuaded some of my own staff, like Angela Hartnett, to help run things, I was even keener. That kind of sealed it for me – the idea that trusted friends would be at my side.

Then there was the money side of things. I think I had to do something like fifteen nights' live TV. For a show like *Kitchen Nightmares*, I was getting about £5,000 a programme, and I would have worked my arse off for that. But ITV were offering me £40,000 an hour, so I would basically earn half a million pounds for two weeks' work. You can't earn that kind of money as a chef. I'm not saying that I did it for the money, but it certainly helped. At the time, Gordon Ramsay Holdings was evolving and developing, and we'd just taken on a substantial new building in terms of rent, so the thought of getting half a million quid for two weeks' work was extraordinary. Even Chris was slightly taken aback when they came through with that offer.

As was obvious to anyone who caught even five minutes

of the show, I wasn't too impressed when I met the contestants. To be honest, I didn't know who half of them were. I'd never seen the Pub Landlord so Al Murray, the comedian who plays him, was a new face to me. As for Jennifer Ellison, the former *Brookside* actress who went on to win the show – for some reason I had an idea that she was in *Friends*.

Edwina Currie was the face I knew best. It was all a bit weird.

Plus, once they were standing there in front of me, I could see the task was more immense than I had expected. How were this lot going to cook food to a high enough standard to be served in a restaurant? More to the point, how were they going to do it quickly enough?

The programme seemed to have a bit of a curse over it right from the start. The night before we even opened the *Hell's Kitchen* restaurant, Roger Cook, the investigative reporter, fell through his chair and broke his leg. Then Tommy Vance, the DJ, and Roger's replacement, decided he couldn't take the pace, and walked out.

After that, the whole thing was just one long argument. I was furious with the production people for the amount they were allowing the contestants to drink late at night. This might have made some of the footage they got better, but I had a fucking restaurant to run. I felt like we had no control. I said to Angela and Sarge, 'Why are we making them look good when they're giving us so much shit?'

There was a diary room, where contestants could go and whinge and moan to a psychiatrist. Any time it came to prepping vegetables, they'd all fuck off to the diary room. Their attitude to me was: 'Don't pick on us.' But my attitude to them was: you're on a minimum fee of twenty-five to thirty grand for being here. My guys work for fucking twelve months to earn twenty grand. You're here for two weeks and you think that I'm going to kiss your arse? So that was it. The battle lines were drawn. They were all supposed to be cooks, so I treated them like cooks. I expected them to get on and do the job.

After the first night, the ratings were amazing. Something like 9.9 million people watched. And every single one of those people seemed to be saying: fucking hell, have you seen that man in the kitchen? I can't believe he's so fucking rude. Overnight, we lost three million viewers, and then the press were really on my case. The headline writers were really let loose. It was all: 'Ramsay Pushes Too Far' – all that bullshit. Meanwhile I was staying in this little hotel round the corner from the restaurant, which was in Brick Lane. I was getting about two hours sleep a night, and five days of real pounding in the press. And then the contestants started walking out, and I found myself thinking: we've got a week to run yet. Will anyone still be here in one week's time? Everyone had totally different agendas. It was chaos. Total chaos.

The real problem with the show was the huge gap

between my expectations and that of the producers and the contestants. The producers were only worried about making a 'reality' TV programme, and the contestants were only worried about how they looked on that programme, whereas I was attempting to run a proper, fine-dining restaurant. In some sense, I felt that my reputation was on the line. They thought this was the foodie equivalent of *I'm a Celebrity ... Get Me Out Of Here!* But out in a jungle, there are places you can hide. In a kitchen, there's nowhere to hide. As for Angus Deayton, who was presenting the show, he and Danny Baker were supposed to be writing the scripts together at first, but then they had some kind of big argument and Baker walked. So Angus was on his own, and I soon found out that he was taking the piss out of me. He was so sarcastic. I had a little dugout I could sit in with a chair and a sofa and a fridge with Lucozade in it. Angus had this fucking great big caravan outside in the car park. He'd swan up with his script early evening, and all I could think was: I've been here since six o'clock this morning. They wanted me to chat to Angus on camera – you know, a bit of friendly camaraderie – but the show was live, so they couldn't make me. He was fucked then. 'Fuck off, Angus,' I could say. 'I'm not interested. I'm too busy.'

I went to ITV and I said: you're going to have to radically change something. You're going to have to get some prep chefs in – these people aren't professional chefs and they're in danger of collapsing. Then came my big confrontation with Amanda Barrie, the *Coronation Street* actress.

She was convinced that the whole thing was some kind of set-up, that the contestants were being carefully stage-managed. This thought festered away in her paranoid mind until she physically tried to punch me. She meant it, too. I could see it in her eyes. At that point, I walked. I said to ITV: she's going to have to be removed. What are you waiting for? For someone to be stabbed? My walking never came out in the press, but let me tell you now, all hell was let loose.

Also, something really awful had happened in the toilet of the restaurant. A customer had got so drunk that she had collapsed there. When she woke up, she accused the security guard who'd found her there of trying to rape her. So, all of a sudden, at 3.30 in the morning, the place was cordoned off and covered in police and basically about to be shut down. In the end, it turned out that the woman had just lost her mother; she left the country the next day, and neither she nor the police pursued it. The whole fucking thing had basically gone tits up.

That night, I walked all the way home to Wandsworth from Brick Lane. I went straight down the Embankment, still in my chef's whites. I think they had various cars out looking for me. It was really weird. I felt completely spaced out.

I thought: if they're not going to listen to me, I'm not

going to do this any more. The contestants were dropping like flies, and ITV just wouldn't accept it. The next day, on the Sunday, there was no morning roll-call of the contestants as usual because I just didn't show up. At which point, ITV finally agreed to give them Sunday off, and to get some prep chefs in. And so I agreed to go back. However, even though I'd arranged for these so-called celebrities to be given a bit of a break, I wasn't going to be treated like shit by them. I wasn't going to spend my days massaging their egos. No way.

Jennifer Ellison, who eventually won the show, worked well, no doubt about it. So did Al Murray. He was the only one who'd write everything down, who got up in the morning, who didn't hang around drinking all night. There was a level of respect there, and quite a lot of talent. To this day, he puts on amazing dinner parties. He's a fucking good cook. He takes it seriously. He's able to lose himself in it.

Abi Titmuss was just totally hilarious, really. All she really wanted to do was flirt and argue. She wouldn't be told. In the end, I just thought: I don't care.

Of course, the one who really got on my tits was Edwina Currie. That was a tough one. There were members of the public, and even quite a few of my mates, voting to keep her in the show just because they loved watching her wind me up. When the show was over, one of my friends admitted to me that he'd spent £400 trying to keep her in. She was just so fucking lazy and totally irritating. The way she used to rabbit on in French to me. She knew I hated her constant whingeing.

The occasion for the big bust-up came when she didn't prepare her special. Throughout the day about eight different people had come up to me, warning me that she hadn't prepared it. My attitude was: I don't care. They knew I was going to flip my lid, and so did I. But I wasn't going to get on her case and provide her with a get-out-of-jail-free card. I didn't give two fucks that we were going to be a dish short. We'd make do.

So, the hour arrived. It was about ten minutes past six when I said to Edwina: 'Where's your special? What are you doing today?'

'I haven't done it,' she said. It was supposed to be guinea fowl.

'Say that again.'

'It's not really my dish, and I don't like it, so I haven't done it.'

The production people were going mad. They didn't want to lose any more contestants. But I didn't give a fuck. We would struggle on regardless.

I looked at her and I said: 'You're a fucking joke, aren't you?'

'I beg your pardon?'

'One minute you are shagging the prime minister and now you are trying to shag me from behind.'

It just came out. I hadn't planned it at all. I knew how much she was getting paid. I knew how everyone was running around kissing her arse, totally scared of her. Well, I was not scared of Edwina Currie – a bully who shagged the prime minister. It was music to my ears when she finally got kicked out. The silly cow.

I was hugely relieved when the whole thing was over. I went to the wrap party out of politeness to say thank you to the team and there was Amanda Barrie's girlfriend, giving me more grief. Pathetic. Then I was doubly glad it was over. Three days later, I was off to South Africa to run a double marathon. I pulled out after six hours. My legs were fucked. That was the first time I'd failed to finish a race, and it was all because of Edwina Currie. I was just exhausted. Nothing there.

Soon afterwards, we had an e-mail from Channel 4 saying that they wanted to do a second series of *Kitchen Nightmares*. The retainer they were going to pay me leapt from £50,000 to £100,000. I was amazed. Then ITV asked me if I would do a second series of *Hell's Kitchen*. They put a massive deal on the table. We heard that Fox in America were interested in the idea of doing the show and ITV were telling me that they could sell it around the world. So I was off on a plane to LA to meet Fox, and two days after that, Channel 4 came in with a million-pound offer to keep me there. In the end, I did do the show for Fox – I've done two series, and I'm contracted to do more – but I passed on the offer from ITV in the UK. Why? Lots of reasons. I was really pleased with *Kitchen Nightmares*. I was really excited by it. Whereas *Hell's Kitchen* didn't make so much sense to me. I worried about the way it made people think about me, about the kind of attention it brought.

When it was aired, everyone just piled in. There was my uncle in Scotland doing a fucking live broadcast from outside his pie shop, there were tabloid journalists trawling through my entire history. All the publicity was so negative. On GMTV, they set up this mobile cart outside the restaurant to feed all the customers who were sick of waiting around for their order to arrive. The show attracted lots of knobs, like the coughing Major from *Who Wants to Be a Millionaire?* He started giving me shit at the hotplate. On ITV2, Jordan was presenting the coverage. Hilarious. There she was, walking up and down this red carpet, reading from a card held right up in front of her fucking nose. 'Hello, and welcome to extra portions from *Hell's Kitchen*.' Laughable, really. Worst of all, on GMTV, there was the squashed Bee Gee himself, Antony Worrall Thompson, analysing my every move, telling everyone how he would have handled service. What a joke: it would have killed him. Of course, he'd have loved a gig like that himself.

I felt I was in danger of becoming a caricature.

So why did I agree to do the same show in America? Simple. It wasn't the same show. Fox did it without using so-called celebrities – the contestants were members of the public who seriously wanted to cook, and the prize for the winner, at least for the second series, was the chance to have their own restaurant, in Las Vegas. (First time around, they won enough to get started in business.) It was much more like the original idea I'd had all the years ago and had pitched to the BBC – a kind of culinary boot camp. In other words, it was a real, tough competition. Also, it didn't go out live, which made things a lot easier, and the restaurant wasn't open every day. And I was responsible for the talent, and I could make all the culinary decisions – like whether we got our carrots from the east coast or the west.

I've now signed for five seasons with Fox. I don't think there's a chef in the world who would have turned down the kind of money they've put into the show. And it has paid off – the ratings are amazing. It's a fantastic success. More importantly, it's given me a profile in the US that I could only dream of before.

Even so, I'm careful of my reputation. I don't want to be remembered as an 'all singing all dancing' celebrity chef. That's the reason why, in spite of an amazing offer from BBC1, I've elected to stay with Channel 4. I need to do shows where the cooking, the food, is the most important thing. I always think about a BBC *Good Food* show I did seven years ago. I was just doing this little demonstration in between some of the twats from *Ready Steady Cook*. I'd driven up the night before, after I'd finished service, and I was knackered and quite nervous. I was thinking, oh my God: a live studio audience of 2,000. I was hardly known then.

As I walked into the green room backstage, and there was Nick Nairn, Antony Worrall Thompson, Paul Rankin and Ainsley Harriott, and they were all half-naked, stripped to their waists. The four of them were getting their backs massaged. Ainsley stretched his arms and said in a patronising manner: 'Remember, it's only showbiz.' My nerves completely disappeared when I heard that. I went out on stage and gave the most amazing demonstration. I just thought: fuck off, will you. Let me do the real cooking.

Talk about celebrity chefs ... Of course, now after my television shows, I'm now part of that strange celebrity world. So much of it is a pile of crap, though. We've had everyone in the restaurants from Pierce Brosnan to Beckham, but we don't have special arrangements for celebrities – there's no secret telephone number for them. We try to ensure their privacy, though that's pretty difficult these days. If people want to go up to them and ask them to sign a napkin, there's nothing we can do about that.

Tana and I have become quite close to the Beckhams – we all spent a New Year's Eve together – and I do get frustrated when people are so wrong about them. When you get to know them, you realise how normal they are – and how normal they want to be. Compared to them, though, I've had it relatively easy from the press. They've been nice to me. The most frustrating thing is the chequebook journalism, when someone's happy to accept money, a mobile phone and an apartment in Spain to fabricate a story. It's frustrating because, though you might get your turn the next week, once the stuff is out, it's out. I try to work with the press as much as I can. You have to look on it as a relationship, but it's a dangerous one.

Because of everything I've done, there are some amazing moments. I get lots of requests – will you come and cook at my house? Name your price, people will say. But I usually have to turn them down. But one request was to cook for Blair and Putin at Downing Street – which was a great thrill. We cooked for fourteen dignitaries downstairs, and then for the ladies upstairs in the flat – which is just like anyone else's flat, you know, with yoghurts in the fridge, etc. The butlers there are amazing – they're the only people I know who probably even have creases on their Y-fronts. It's a fabulous place to cook. You have to bring everything, from your frying pan to your washing-up liquid. But the best thing about that lunch was that Anton Mossiman was doing the canapés for the press!

For Blair and his guests, we did an amazing ham hock terrine, and some fantastic sea bass, followed by treacle tart. There was a split second when I was standing between Blair and Putin – one of those moments when I couldn't help but think how far I'd come. But the Blairs love their food, I'll say that for them. And after that event, I was invited to Chequers for dinner by Cherie, for a charity event. It was lovely.

Another 'how the hell did I get here' moment was taking part in the UNICEF Soccer Aid event in 2006. It was a football game, with an England XI against a Rest of The World XI. The England team was captained by Robbie Williams, and I was the captain of the Rest of The World team. It was Robbie's idea – he's an ambassador for UNICEF. I met him through the restaurant, I think, and he's mad about football. He said: "You're as passionate about football as I am. Yet I'm a singer, and you're a chef, and neither one of us can do what we really love to do the most of all."

It was an extraordinary occasion. It's not every day that you're in the tunnel at Old Trafford with a crowd of 75,000 people outside and Diego Maradona's hands on your shoulders. I was injured, though – I had a tear in my quad, so for the final I only played 45 minutes. Still, to play against Gazza and Tony Adams and Jamie Redknapp . . .

I wasn't nervous until I walked out onto the pitch and heard the crowd. Then I nearly threw up. The atmosphere was fucking incredible. We got the most amazing reception. But then, when we were warming up, we were running up and down the touchline and Alastair Campbell tripped over his own feet and so, after that, everything was alright. Nine million people saw it on live TV. But we thought: well, we can relax now, because Alastair's made a complete tit of himself. They won 2–1, but it was close.

And there's my cookbooks. My first one was hugely elaborate, complex: a work of art, really. Now I see them as very much as working alongside my TV shows: people see how to do the recipe on screen and then, hopefully, they are interested and want to know more, and so go out and buy the book to try things at home.

I do use cookbooks myself – it's a myth that chefs don't. If I've got a slow braising, I'll always refer back to an authority like Escoffier. Chefs, of course, tend to be too obsessed with the 'picture' of a dish. They cook with their eyes, and everything's got to be a work of art. They want a dish to look stunning, and they get turned on when they see that little bit of magic.

I own about 3,500 cookbooks. I pick them up everywhere I go. Lots are given to me, or I'll buy them. I have an account with Books For Cooks, a fantastic shop in Notting Hill.

Some of the new cookbooks are seriously expensive. The latest one from El Bulli, Ferran Adria's amazing restaurant outside Barcelona, was a limited edition coffee table-style book – an amazing object, like a huge black bible. Anyway, that alone must have cost about £250.

Can I learn anything new from all these books? Of course I can. I must have access to over 5,000 dishes. I never need to check times or quantities. You can use a book for inspiration – especially some of the older books, like Escoffier and even Elizabeth David, who's absolutely inspirational – but you can't just learn to cook from books. That's impossible. There has to be some natural flair.

When I do *Kitchen Nightmares*, I visit kitchens up and down the country and it's always the same. You'll see a book on the shelf, and then you'll see a dish that the chef has replicated right down to the very last drop of chocolate sauce, and it'll look fantastic, and then you pick up your fork and dig in and it will taste absolutely rubbish, fucking disgusting. Let me explain: if I took ten cooks from my kitchen, and each made the most amazing coq au vin using the same recipe, you'd end up with ten completely different dishes. It's all about flair and instinct. I can't say that often enough.

Who would I recommend to the home cook? Nigel Slater, without a doubt. His stuff is personal. He's not a chef, he's a cook. He's never come into fashion and he'll never go out of fashion, he has a timeless quality. Simon Hopkinson's *Roast Chicken and Other Stories* was voted most useful cookbook of all time in 2005, but I'm not convinced. No, it's Nigel Slater for me, every time. Good beyond belief.

But it's the restaurants that really do it for me. Aubergine was named after a three-star place in Munich. I loved the name, and I think people are intimidated by aubergines as well as interested in them, so it was aspirational in two kinds of way. And it's memorable. I used to joke that I was hung like an Aubergine . . . but I've stopped that lately. With *maze*, our totally new kind of restaurant where diners order lots of smaller dishes, we wanted to suggest the idea of finding your way around a menu. A lot of people thought we meant 'mace' like the spice, but we did mean *maze*, honestly.

Most of the restaurants are named after the chefs. *Pétrus* is named after the most famous and magnificent Claret in the world, *La Noisette* ('hazelnut' in french) we just thought was memorable – and it only opened last summer and is packed – a huge success. It opened on the former site of Pengelley's, and it seems that we've finally got the right restaurant at that place. We look for a name that rolls off the lips, it has to be completely memorable without ever being too difficult. I think Nobu (the Japanese restaurant with branches in LA, New York and London) has been very clever in that sense, a great example of how a four-letter word can stick. You want a name that is known all over the world. But if the food and the service aren't right, well, of course, the name is entirely irrelevant.

CHAPTER THIRTEEN

NEW YORK,
NEW YORK

IN EARLY JULY 2006, I went to Holyrood Palace in Edinburgh to pick up my OBE from the Queen. I took Mum, Tana, and Megan – three generations of women from the same family. The award means a huge amount to me; it's just a little outside confirmation of how far I've come, that I'm doing okay. But the most important thing about it was that it was awarded to me for my services to the industry; it had nothing to do with my television work. I think that pleased me more than anything. I felt amazingly proud. Afterwards, we had a decent lunch, and then I took my girls shopping in Harvey Nichols. It was the perfect day.

But while meeting the Queen and trying not to fall flat on your face as you walk backwards gives you pause for thought, it's certainly nothing like a full stop. People often ask me whether there'll ever be a day when I've got enough restaurants in my group, and enough Michelin stars under my belt. The answer to both questions is 'no'. As far as the restaurants go, while the quality is maintained, we'll keep on opening. The important thing for people to realise is that the Gordon Ramsay Group isn't a chain. It's a fantastic collection of individual talents. With regards to Michelin stars: Alain Ducasse has got three sets of three-starred restaurants, in New York, Monaco and Paris. So it's definitely possible. That's my goal.

And I predict Thomas Keller, the American chef, will have two lots of three stars. So, if anything, I feel like I'm lagging behind. I'm under-achieving. I look at Ducasse and Keller, and think: I've got work to do. Luckily, I've got time on my side. I've got ten years on them. And my guys want it as well. They are hungry. What people who are cynical about our expansion fail to grasp is that we don't level out, and fizzle: we just get better and better. Mark Sargeant, now at *Claridge's*, is champing at the bit; if we open a restaurant in Prague, he'll set it up. Stuart Gillies, who's at *Boxwood Café*, we might send to Amsterdam. Angela will open in Florida and, if that's a success, she'll head to New York as well.

Ah, yes. New York. The restaurant capital of the world. Our first restaurant in that fantastic city, *Gordon Ramsay at The London*, opened in November 2006, and making a success of it is going to be the biggest, most important challenge of my career so far. As the song goes, if you can make it there, you can make it anywhere. I intend to make it there – and no one is going to be able to stop me, though, of course, they'll have a damn good try.

'We can't wait to see you go down in flames in New York,' said one anonymous e-mail I received. 'We want the meat off your bones.'

The target in New York is three stars. The American Michelin Guide comes out in November, so after we open, we'll have one year to pull it off.

Do I think we can do it? Fuck me, yes, definitely. The restaurant is amazing. The ingredients you can get your hands on in New York are outstanding. The competition is going to be great chefs like Daniel Boulud and Jean-Georges Vongerichten. But since they won't give a fuck what I'm up to, I'm going to try not to give a fuck about what they're up to either.

New York is a huge gamble. The budget was set at $2.5m, and costs have already risen to $6m. The excitement is already building to the point where I can hardly think of anything else. But I can feel the ideas building inside me, and I know the critics and customers alike are going to be knocked out.

Our American PR agent suggested that we let her arrange an advisory tasting panel before we opened. I sat and listened to her, perfectly politely, and then I said: 'No disrespect, but I'm thirty-nine years old, and I already have three Michelin stars in London. Do you think I'm not ready for scrutiny? Let me tell you this: I'm not sticking my arse out of the Empire State Building so you can all come and poke it. It doesn't work like that. Trust me.'

What I'm trying to say is: I'm ready for New York. I'm ready for anything.

People often ask me about the way eating habits have changed in the years since I became a chef. I always say the same thing: yes, they have, but there's a mammoth task ahead. We had an approach from a huge supermarket recently, to endorse their latest range of ready meals. When we turned it down, the schmuck in charge had the temerity to send us an e-mail telling us how one of the dishes in question has sales of £2 million a week, and how stupid we were not to endorse it. This kind of stuff scares me. For every step forwards, we take ten backwards. The super-markets are still so powerful, and eating habits essentially still so lazy.

I'm not convinced that people cook enough, however many food-related books they buy, or TV shows they watch. I recently ran a campaign to get British families to eat Sunday lunch together again, so this is something that I've thought about a lot. The truth is, we've all got too much money now, and you see this at every level. Most of the young chefs who come into my kitchen expect to start on salaries of £25,000; that's what they think they need to survive. I think money, far from encouraging creativity in the kitchen, has somehow stifled it. We need to get our feeling for ingredients, for running a kitchen budget back.

We need to get closer to what we eat, to scrutinise it more, to love it and pay it attention.

So far, whatever anyone likes to think, the food revolution in this country has largely been limited to London. There are exceptions to this rule, but not many. Look at France, the way food there is still so regional. You go to Lyon, Brittany, Bordeaux, Aix-en-Provence or Champagne, and you'll know where you are through the food you're eating. It's extraordinary. So anyone who goes on about how the restaurants in London are now better than the restaurants in Paris should compare the places you can find in Chelmsford with their equivalents twenty-five miles outside Paris. We are miles behind, fucking miles. Go to a French service station. You'll get guinea fowl with lentils, or fantastic lamb with flageolet beans. Little Chefs don't employ CHEFS; they employ people who can use the technology they've installed to heat up pre-prepared food. And yet Little Chefs have queues outside them – QUEUES. If that's not depressing, I don't know what is.

But that's not to say that I'm not hopeful that things will get better, slowly and surely – and I'm willing to play any part I can in making British habits change. As you must know by now, I think good food is important. It can be life-changing. Just look what it's done for me.

CHAPTER FOURTEEN
FAMILY

IT'S BEEN ALMOST A YEAR since I finished work on the first edition of *Humble Pie*, and it's been one of the most amazing years of my life. I don't mean professionally, though life in the many kitchens I run around the world just gets better and better: it's more that writing my story has changed everything – the way I feel about my life, the way I look at the world, even the way I talk to certain members of my family. It has, in short, lightened my load.

I feel that what I put inside the pages of *Humble Pie* has lifted a monkey from my back. It's as though I've cleared out all my dustiest closets, and no one can hurt me any more. The stories that used, occasionally, to appear in the newspapers – the ones that would go on about why I was so firm and assertive, vicious even, during my days at Aubergine – won't happen any longer and, even if they did, they would be pointless.

There's nothing anyone can say about me now that I haven't said about myself already. It's all here, in these pages, laid bare. I have faced up to my ghosts and, in doing so, I have finally won the long battle with my past. I can put it behind me now in a way I could never before. It's such a huge relief.

After *Humble Pie* was published, I received an unbelievable number of letters. The book signings I did were extraordinary too. So many people. Taunton, which is where Mum lives, especially sticks in my mind. It was mayhem there.

What did my family make of it? After all, in many ways, it was their story I was telling just as much my own. Mum couldn't put it down; she sat up half the night reading it. I was anxious about how it would make her feel, but I needn't have worried. This book, combined with the major heart surgery she underwent, seems to have changed the way she deals with the world. She's more assertive, less soft. I feel incredibly proud of her.

Her latest campaign is to try and get Diane to stop smoking. She has the zeal of the convert, so far as smoking goes. She also dealt with my uncle Ronald, my father's brother, who was livid about how I portrayed Dad. I had a really shitty e-mail from his son, my cousin, so that was all very fragile for a while. There are still problems between Yvonne and me. But we'll get through them. I'd like her to make up with Mum first, because Mum is at the top of all this. We'll see . . . I even think that *Humble Pie* helped Diane get closer to her partner, Trevor. I don't think she'd ever really been able to tell him what had happened to her as a child. But now he knows it all, and I think that has given him a new understanding of her.

What about Ronnie? When *Humble Pie* came out, I told the world that I'd washed my hands of him. I didn't know where he was or what he was doing, apart from the fact that he was dabbling with the tabloids and, I assumed, back on the drugs. I said that it was over between me and him: I couldn't take any more. The trouble is that blood will always run thicker than water. Fuck, he's my little brother. What can you do? At the end of last year, I got a phone call from him. It was pretty frosty, but he got it all off his chest. He felt that he'd been exploited. His point was that my book had left him with nothing – that I'd exposed him, that now he would never be able to get a job. Which was fucking ridiculous. For one thing, it was already widely known that Ronnie had been both a heroin addict and in trouble with the law; it wasn't like it was a secret. But I also resented his tone. He kept telling me that my support had to be 'unconditional'.

Putting aside the fact that the only condition I ever attached to my support for him was that he stayed off the drugs, which seemed fair enough in the circumstances, I just hated the self-centredness of this. So when was I allowed to hurt? When did I get to scream from the fucking rooftops?

Who was I supposed to talk to? I swear there were times when Ronnie's behaviour used to have such a profound effect on me that I just wanted to do something wild – you know, like sky-dive from an aeroplane or something. I needed some kind of release. I couldn't believe that he couldn't grasp this. But, no.

'You sold my story,' he accused. Addicts are selfish; it's always, ALWAYS about them.

Anyway, it got really ugly. I went to pick him up in my car, and suddenly he was telling me that he'd got this girl-friend from Thailand.

'Listen, Ron,' I said. 'Is she a working girl?'

'No, no, no.'

Apparently, he was off to meet her in Knightsbridge so I dropped him off there. The next thing I knew, he was off telling the tabloids that she was actually a high-class call girl, and that I'd gone into the building with him. This story didn't actually make the newspapers, of course, it was too fucking ridiculous. But it disgusted me that we had to make it clear to these journalists that Ronnie was still using, and that whatever money they were giving him – or planning on giving him – would be spent on funding his habit. They were offering him extraordinary sums: £40,000, £100,000. I saw the draft contracts.

When he got in touch again, I asked him what he wanted. 'I want to go back to Indonesia,' he said. 'I can find my soul there.' I told him that I would help, but that there was no way I would pay for him to go through rehab all over again, and I wanted him to be clean.

So he went off to Bali. At first he was apparently helping to build a new dive centre, after which he was working as a chef in a café-bar. Then the line went dead after that.

I hadn't given him any funding on this occasion. I paid for his ticket out there, and his first month's accommodation. That's all. Last time he went out there, he was ringing me every day, and reversing the charges. This time, I told him that he could ring once a week. I was always preparing to assume the brace position so far as Ronnie goes and the level of anxiety was fucking unbelievable. And then, when I did speak to him, it was like walking on egg shells. I tried not to sound negative, or ask how work was going, or whether or not he'd had a beer. The last time we went through this, he insisted that he could handle a beer. This time, he was insisting that he was no longer interested in drinking even one. That should have tipped me the wink that a storm was on the way.

Just before the tsunami hit me I had a call from Ronnie with one of his only too plausible requests for £1,200 for an English teaching course. I wired over the money and two weeks later I asked him how the course was going. He told me that unfortunately the price of the course had gone up and he hadn't been able to enrol. 'So where's the money?', I asked. He told me that he had a few debts to pay off and that there wasn't anything left. I felt so, so stupid.

The call comes through late one night when I'm fast asleep in my bed. It's Ronnie. It's going to be bad news. The tsunami has hit.

He starts a long rigmarole about how he has been set up and that someone had handed him a fix just before the police arrived. Long and the short, Ronnie, my fucking nuisance, useless brother, has got himself locked up in a Balinese jail on drugs charges. Didn't he realise that these people don't muck around when it comes to drugs?

I know no one in Bali. I have no understanding of how legal procedures operate, how someone gets representation and, most terrifying what the likely sentences may be if Ronnie is found guilty. How can the little bastard dump these problems on me after I have tried so hard in the past?

The story is just so full of holes and the most obvious question is how is he able to speak to me on a mobile if he is in a jail? Whose mobile is it and who is paying for it? Am I being set up once again? He already has a number for me to call which will get me through to a lawyer.

I pass this information over to Chris who is on holiday at present, and tell Ronnie that I shall get back to him as soon as I can. Chris calls the lawyer who says that it is all a matter of money. Probably about US$50,000 to get Ronnie out within six months. Otherwise it could be ten years in jail. Chris thanks him and reports back to me with the suggestion that he also contacts the British Consulate in Bali.

The Consulate representative is very helpful but has no ready answers. What we need is real information and someone we can trust out there to find out what really is happening. Chris contacts Mark Stables, previously employed to baby-sit Ronnie when he last came out of rehab. Mark is an Australian but knows his way around places like Bali and is familiar with all sorts of people. Thankfully he agrees to go out there immediately to find out whatever he can.

In the meantime the calls keep coming in from Ronnie. He is moaning about the conditions and wants to know what I am doing about it all. If I do nothing, he tells me, he will go to the newspapers. He has now confessed to me that he has been using for some time and I am devastated by this news. He is never going to be clean and after all that everyone has been through, after all the horrendous sums of money that have been spent on his recovery, I now know that it has all been for nothing. Thank you, Ronnie.

Mark Stables is under strict instructions on his way out not to make contact with Ronnie as this is a fact-finding trip and I just need to know what is really going on.

I decide to talk it all through with Diane and Mum, particularly now we know that Ronnie wasn't framed after all but is back on drugs. We have tried everything and I know Mum in particular is at her wits' end. It sounds like the only way we are going to get Ronnie out of Bali is to find someone who can bribe their way through the system and I don't think that we are prepared to do this any more. What happens if Ronnie is let out in a few months? He will become our collective responsibility again and his skills at manipulating one part of the family against the other know no bounds. Tough Love is the only way to go and I think that we all know this. Ronnie is a bad lot and he has chosen this route. I think that we all agree that we must withdraw from the front line and let Bali dispense their own justice.

Ronnie keeps to his threat of going to the newspapers and on 11th March 2007 there is a double page spread in the *Sunday Mirror* headlined, 'Exclusive: My Bali jail hell by £60m Ramsay's junkie brother'. The bulk of one page is taken up with a picture of Ronnie behind bars, posing like he's in a scene from Jailhouse Rock. Aren't these newspapers wonderful? He has a mobile phone and he can pose for pictures in his cell. He even talked about giving press conferences. It is all very difficult to understand.

One of the biggest revelations contained in *Humble Pie* was the news that I had discovered that somewhere out there I had a half-sister – the result of a fling my father had as a teenager. I didn't know this woman's name, or where she lived, or indeed anything else about her and, as you've just read, I had never tried to find her for fear of hurting my mother. I was in two minds about including this in the book. For one thing, I had to be prepared for the fact that this announcement might attract gold-diggers and publicity seekers, all busy claiming to share my DNA. I could just imagine it: 'I looked in the mirror, and suddenly saw Gordon Ramsay looking right back at me!' For another – and this was much more serious – there was the chance that my REAL sister would come forward, and then I would have to deal with the idea of meeting her. Was I really prepared for that? I think I was, though I wanted the whole family to be there – especially, Mum – and I wanted the encounter to take place in private, far from the glare of the cameras. So my little surprise wasn't edited out. I published, and I waited, with bated breath.

It wasn't long before the fallout began. *Humble Pie* was published at the end of September 2006. Just days later, the *Mail on Sunday* had the story: there was my secret sister, Sharon Donnachie, a 43-year-old mother-of-two who works in a bookshop at Glasgow Airport, living in a two-bedroom council flat on the outskirts of the city. The newspaper made a lot of the fact that this flat was 'sparsely furnished' (whereas I, of course, was in possession of a vast fortune). It also noted that: 'the distinctive lines on her face are unmistakeable'. Her mother, Margaret Miller, had died in a cancer hospice 12 years previously. Her half-brother, now 33, was living in Australia. She was understandably delighted to find that she had a whole new lot of relatives, one of whom – yours truly – she had apparently long admired from afar.

I looked at the photograph. It's true: Sharon Donnachie does look a lot like me: same wrinkles, same nose, same hair. But I couldn't help but feel queasy. How had the newspaper got hold of her? It upset me. It felt like too much. For her part, it wasn't the right thing to do. I'd wanted to meet her in private, on my own terms. Now here she was in a national newspaper, saying: 'All this time I've been watching his shows, particularly *Hell's Kitchen*, and thinking how fabulous he is – and the man I've been admiring is my brother.'

It seemed that she had known that she might have relatives on her missing father's side, but that she had never felt able to try and find out, partly because she thought of her stepfather, Thomas Donnachie, as her father. 'I never really felt able to trace my family,' she said in the interview. 'I always knew what had happened to my mum, but things were different in those days and people didn't speak about such things. My stepfather said my real father had passed away, so I just left it. I didn't know his name until the *Mail on Sunday* told me.' Could that be right? Had the newspaper contacted her? Or had she got in touch with them? Either way, I wasn't happy. I couldn't understand why, if she really did want to meet all of us, she hadn't been a little more discreet about it. It was eerie.

That's the word for it – eerie. Why couldn't she just have written me a quiet note? This was real life – hers and mine – not some stupid publicity stunt. It was cheap.

The following Sunday, things only got worse. The newspaper followed up its scoop by trying to prove that Sharon

Donnachie shared some sort of mysterious cooking gene with me. Fucking ridiculous. Cooking's not like being left-handed, or able to roll your tongue. It's a fucking skill, learnt like any other. The paper had arranged for her to have the 'run of the kitchen' at a Glasgow restaurant called Red Onion, where the chef is John Quigley. Under Quigley's gaze, she produced 'a char-grilled chicken and pesto spaghetti dish fit for any celebrity chef'. Beneath this pathetic cook-off was a recipe for 'Sharon's celebrity chicken spaghetti'. 'I absolutely love to cook, and always have done,' she was quoted as saying. 'I suppose I'm a perfectionist, just like Gordon, and I hate it when anything goes wrong – although I never shout and swear like he does. With John's help, I think I've come up with something which I could offer to Gordon to eat, although I admit I'll be embarrassed to cook for such a culinary genius.' I thought this was incredibly tacky – of her, and of the *Mail on Sunday*. She was even photographed wearing a chef's jacket. Fucking hell. It was too much.

I thought: get real, will you? It looked to me like the newspaper had taken Sharon, who obviously knew nothing of the press, for a ride. It's hard to explain. I don't scare easily, but this episode really unnerved me. And worse, thereafter every time I went to Scotland, the newspapers would suggest that I was 'ignoring' my new sister by not visiting her. They accused me of one slight after another. This was total fucking rubbish. How can I be ignoring someone whom I've never even met before? Meanwhile, poor old Diane was upset because she thought that Sharon looked more like me than she did. I couldn't really reassure her about this. It was true. Genes work in mysterious ways.

The upshot of all this is that I haven't met Sharon – yet. In spite of everything, I do feel as though I want to. But when I do, it will be totally private and on my own terms. The point being that I won't be doing it on my own. This, like everything else, is about Mum. I have to be very careful. I'd never want to upset her. What Dad did must have hurt: it would have hurt any woman. Luckily, Mum is not the kind of person to bear grudges. When it finally happens, I think she'll cope. But I certainly don't wish that I'd cut the story of Sharon from my original manuscript.

There is a funny postscript to all this. Well, it's funny now. It certainly wasn't at the time. I was in Melbourne in Australia, doing publicity, signing books. Suddenly, some-one came up rushing up to me. 'Your brother's here,' they said. Fuck. My heart was flipping over something crazy. Who was about to come out of the woodwork now? Or did they mean Ronnie? I looked over. 'That's not my brother,' I said. It was actually Sharon's Australian half-brother. In other words, no relation to me at all. Even so, I avoided a meeting. 'Take his details,' I asked someone. 'I'll call him.' But when I did, he got upset with me – he couldn't understand why I hadn't wanted to meet him. I just can't win, can I?

CHAPTER FIFTEEN

THE IMPORTANT
THINGS IN LIFE

On December 19th, 2006, I flew out to Afghanistan, to cook Christmas dinner for the British troops based at Camp Bastion in Helmand Province. With me were two of my most trusted lieutenants, Angela Hartnett and Jason Atherton, and my father-in-law, Chris. in conjunction with the Ministry of Defence and the *Daily Mirror*. I'd been planning this trip for some time. Still, nothing prepares you for the reality. Watching the TV news is one thing, flying into Helmand Province, one of the bleakest and most dangerous places on earth, is quite another. We went from RAF Brize Norton in an ageing Tri-Star along with our kit and body armour. It was heavy and uncomfortable and just looking at it was enough to scare the shit out of you.

En route, we stopped in Germany, picking up some Marines, and then flew on to Kandahar.

From Kandahar we flew down to Camp Bastion in a Hercules. It was like being inside a giant lorry. Just before our descent, we put on our helmet and body armour. It was bloody uncomfortable and restrictive. Everyone was armed but it was only when we were approaching the base that what we were about to do really hit home. These 18-year-old soldiers were all around us, ready, focused and just incredibly disciplined. And you're sitting in darkness because of the danger of mortar attack, on a sudden and rapid descent like nothing I'd ever experienced before.

The flight was only 40 minutes long and it turned out that our Captain for that flight had celebrated his wedding anniversary at *Claridge's*, and so he asked me if I wanted to sit in the cockpit. It was amazing. 'We're going in,' he said, and the plane just shot down between the mountains. We heard explosions around us, but we were safely out of reach. They can make between nine and twelve flights like this each night. It's very humbling. You see the racks where the stretchers go that bring back injured men, and you think: this is not Singapore Airlines, this is not fucking first class. It hits you in the chest: fuck me, this is real. And then you get out, and you're in the middle of nowhere, and it's dark and freezing cold, and you can forget your fucking mobile phone. The Hercules has to get going straight away. They can't sit on the ground so you have to make swift work of getting out onto what passes for a runway. Basically you're tipped out, and from then on you're in another world.

By the time we arrived, it was about 5.30 a.m. We went to meet the officers, and they showed us the first galley, in which we planned to cook the Christmas dinner for 800 men. It was on the back of a Land Rover – not exactly what I was used to. The second galley was a little better – it was in a tent – but the ovens were about the size of microwaves, and there was just no way that we would be able to get them hot enough to roast turkeys.

That was the first blow. The second came when we inquired about the supplies we had ordered. The trucks that travel to Camp Bastion with supplies run the risk of being attacked by the Taliban, even though they're driven by Afghans. They're known as 'jingle-jangle lorries', and only half of them make it through. Once they do arrive, they have to sit two kilometres out from the camp for 24 hours as a security measure in case they're rigged with bombs or carrying suicide bombers. Sniffer dogs check them out.

Anyway, the truck that made it through the day we arrived had had half its carriage blown away after coming under attack. Nor did it seem to be carrying any of the supplies that we'd ordered. No fresh vegetables to speak of. No chillies for the harissa I'd been planning on making, and no pumpkins for the soup. No tomatoes either. But it is not the place to be downhearted. For one thing, an officer made it clear we were lucky to have anything at all. 'We busted a gut to get the stuff you see in front of you,' he said. 'We haven't seen anything like this since we came out here.' For another, I had a sense that, however tough it was going to be, we could really make a difference to the men's day. I'd had no sleep, but the adrenalin was pumping around my body. 'You might be the CEO of a company that's turning £50m,' I said to Chris, 'but that doesn't mean anything out here. You and any spare Marines you can find had better start peeling the bloody potatoes.'

An officer warned us that we had a long day ahead – perhaps we wanted to get our heads down. We didn't, but we did go to our quarters to have a shower. I was glad to see that we were in the same tent as the Marines. Trust me, there were no special arrangements. Out there, it doesn't matter a fuck who you are. Around the tent encampment were blast protectors to absorb mortar attacks should any take place. Inside, the Marines were still sleeping. At 6 a.m., it was time for the Marines to get up. It was hilarious, watching them pull back the curtain on the shower only to find Angela standing there. There aren't many women who would have mucked in like that, but she didn't give a fig. Like me, she just wanted to get the job done.

Back to the food. There was obviously no way that we could roast the birds so we steamed the breasts and then roasted them, smeared in butter, one at a time. Then I boned out all the legs, and stuffed them with couscous. About a dozen Marines were helping us, plus a few officers. I went off to the dry store where I found some bacon and spaghetti, some dried oregano and basil, tinned tomatoes and stock cubes. I could make minestrone soup! Even better, with the addition of a bit of curry powder, they would be able to use the leftovers the next day too, for mulli-gatawny. 'This soup has got legs!', I told them.

The potatoes we roasted on what amounted to a giant barbecue. We made some stuffing from sausage meat, which we roasted with some sage in these giant frying pans, and some dried apricots, also taken from the dry store. That was then sliced up. We did chipolatas, and cabbage braised with onions. We'd brought honey and cloves and brown sugar with us, so that we could do a fantastic honey-baked ham. "Everyone will have a choice," I said to the officer. "You can forget that," came the reply. "They'll eat every-thing at the same time." He was right, of course. You should have seen their plates, stacked high with two main courses. And then, once they'd finished that, they'd come back up for soup. We'd also brought 1,000 mince pies and goody bags filled with Christmas treats donated by Philip Green of Top Shop and BHS fame. They had also contained a miniature of Scotch and a Christmas cracker but these had to be removed on the insistence of the MOD. Within min-utes, I'd forgotten all about New York, where we'd just opened our new restaurant. The stress and the glamour seemed a million miles away. Being in Helmand Province gave me the most amazing sense of perspective.

The food taken care of, the men showed us various aspects of camp life. We were taken out in the tanks to visit the watchmen in their bunkers. They work in shifts of fours, two hours on and two hours off, with one of them asleep at any one time. We took some lunch out to them, and they were extraordinary guys doing an extraordinary job. Next, I met the bomb disposal team, and got to dress up in their gear and explode some bombs myself. After that, I went out on the range and did some target practice with small arms. My hands were shaking like you wouldn't believe and the kickback was amazing. Then I climbed into an Apache helicopter. Incredible. You put on goggles that aim the firepower to wherever direction you are looking. This is not part of the world that I'm used to.

Finally, they wanted me to put on a padded suit and run away from a specially trained Alsatian. I think they wanted to have a bit of fun at my expense, and why not? I can't say I was keen, but you don't say no out there. You just get on with it. They warned me that once the dog caught up with me, as it inevitably would, it would nip. When I put the suit on, I noticed there was a hole in it. 'There's a hole there,' I said, feebly. 'Shut the fuck up,' said the soldier. Angela and Jason, needless to say, were wetting themselves with laughter. 'GO!' someone shouted. At which point I fucking bolted. I'll outrun the thing, I thought. Some hope. The dog was soon on me. They're vicious – easily capable of ripping off an arm or a leg. It knocked me for six, and I'm a big guy. Did they call it off? Did they fuck! They took their time. It felt like an age.

The bond you feel out there was phenomenal. The men were buoyant, always cracking jokes in spite of the enormous difficulty of their task, or the fact that some of their colleagues had lost their lives. This meant that, far from being relieved to be leaving, I felt quite sad, although for a time it was far from certain that we would get home in time for Christmas Day. There were security alerts and mortar bombs and there was every chance that we would be stranded. But then we heard that a young man had been injured when his jeep had fallen into a sudden dip. He'd broken a vertebra and needed to be flown out urgently. In the end, we accompanied him and left in a C17, a huge plane that is like a flying hangar.

It's in a place like Afghanistan that the world steadies itself for me. I had been worrying endlessly about what Frank Bruni, the food critic of the *New York Times*, was going to say about our new restaurant. Suddenly, I couldn't give a damn about Bruni, or any of his type. There are far more important things in life. When I got home, Megan, my eldest daughter, noticed a burn on my arm. She was obsessed that I'd been shot. I thought about how lucky we are as a family – safe and well. I could reassure her, and that felt so good.

There are a few people that I wouldn't mind taking out to Afghanistan. This is going to make me sound old for my years, but I think that we need to bring back military service. It would do everyone the world of good: the bond, the camaraderie, the discipline. Life is too easy for most of us, too idyllic, too comfortable. The guys I met out there were coming in for breakfast looking completely immaculate –

boots shining, clothes crisp. They were 'ready' and I was impressed.

I've agreed that my trip won't be a one-off. We were grafting. It was hard work, no one had any sleep, but we made a difference. If I'm honest, I would have paid to go out there. So I'll be back next Christmas. I'm absolutely determined to make it happen. Stand by your ovens, guys!

I turned 40 in 2006, and celebrated with a party in the Banqueting House on Whitehall, London for 250 guests. It was fantastic: Matthew Pinsent was there, along with Jeremy Clarkson, Piers Morgan, Kirsty Young, Ron Dennis and even my old sparring partner, Michael Winner. David Beckham, alas, was locked in a hotel room preparing for a game. Rory Bremner kicked the evening off with some stand-up; the cast of *Chicago* played; and a burlesque artist was there on a rocking-horse, looking, well, fucking burlesque. Amazing. Dinner was lobster thermidor, followed by rib eye steak with béarnaise sauce, hand-cut chips and Caesar salad. We finished with a winter berry crumble. Then, at midnight, just in case anyone was still hungry, we served breakfast. It's a bit of a blur, though I do remember the presents: they were just endless. Best present of all? A 1927 rectangular Rolex from my parents-in-law. It's beautiful. On the day of my birthday itself, Tana and I had lunch at Cipriani London, and dinner at Le Gavroche. I couldn't think of a better place to spend the evening: Le Gavroche means so much to me in food terms, and Albert [Roux] served wines from 1966 – Mouton Rothschild, Chateau Latour. Incredible wines. It was a perfect evening.

But there's more to celebrate than just turning 40. A lot more. The past twelve months, for all that I've barely had a day off, have been extraordinary. The big event, of course, was New York. I knew it would be intense, taking on Manhattan, but I didn't realise quite HOW intense. What they say is true: if you can make it there, you can make it anywhere. It was hard not to feel paranoid. The last time I felt under this much scrutiny was when I opened Aubergine. First, the stories started appearing in the press: our neighbours were unhappy with the noise and the mess, I'd been sacking staff, I was in trouble with the unions. It was all rubbish, mostly. I did sack staff, but only those who were drinking my cellar dry and entertaining girls from Las Vegas, or who just weren't up to the job. Then there were the critics. *Time Out* and the *New York Observer* both gave us amazing reviews. *New York* magazine and *The New York Times* didn't, and that was a kick in the bollocks.

But I know that the food is amazing, and the room is one of the most beautiful in the world. Frank Bruni, the *New York Times* critic came in at least five times, and was forever trying to catch us out. His guests would be late, and he'd ask us if keeping the table would be a problem – that kind of thing. He'd pickled my bollocks before his review even came out. On his blog, he complained that customers were forever taking photos. Well, my point is this: a lot of people save up all year to go to a restaurant like ours. It would be pretty fucking arrogant to refuse them a photo if they ask.

I think the real problem is that some critics are judging me rather than the food. They don't like *Hell's Kitchen*, or *Kitchen Nightmares*, and it all gets very personal. What really amazes me, though, is that in New York, there are legions of amateur critics, all blogging away, posting pictures they've surreptitiously – or not so surreptitiously – taken with their camera phones. Luckily, the people that really count, the public, seem to love it. The place is full. I've got letters from customers who just can't understand the bad reviews. Still, I take criticism on the chin. You can always improve, and you've got to keep your eye on the ball. Since we opened, both Alain Ducasse and Thomas Keller have been in – great, Michelin-starred chefs the pair of them – and they both reminded me that there's no point paying too much attention to negative personality stuff. What counts is the cooking.

Meanwhile, the business continues to expand. By the time you read this, Angela Hartnett, who received an MBE in the 2007 New Year's Honours list, will have opened her restaurant in Miami. I know it will be fantastic. In October, we open our first restaurant in France – it's in Versailles – which is going to be a serious business. I'm less well-known as a personality in France, which is a relief. But any Englishman who cooks in France, as I know from bitter experience, is going to be on the receiving end of some stern treatment. The food is going to have to be better than perfect. Does it feel like I'm rolling my tanks onto their lawn? A bit. It's fucking exciting, though. In January 2008, we open in Los Angeles, followed by Prague, Amsterdam and then Dublin. Our group will then consist of fifteen world-class restaurants. Do I have enough hot young talent to feed this expansion? You bet I do. Big time. In France, I may even put a woman chef in the kitchen. Let's see what they make of that.

In London, our reputation only grows. When the Michelin ratings were announced in January 2007, we held on to all our existing stars (Restaurant *Gordon Ramsay* has three; Angela Hartnett at *The Connaught*, *maze*, *The Savoy Grill* and Gordon Ramsay at *Claridge's* all have one), and Marcus Wareing at *Pétrus* in The Berkeley Hotel went up to two stars. I knew it would happen – I would have been gobsmacked if it hadn't – and I couldn't be happier for him. The only disappointment is that Jason Atherton at *maze* didn't also go up to two. But it's just a matter of time: I know he'll get there. And then there is *La Noisette*, which occupies the site of the now defunct Pengelley's. We back *La Noisette*, and its chef, Bjorn van der Horst, formerly of The Greenhouse. He also picked up a star and, in doing so, helped to lay to rest the ghost of Pengelley's, a disaster which we have been glad to put behind us.

My television career goes from strength to strength. We won an Emmy for *Hell's Kitchen US*, and now we have signed a deal to do *Kitchen Nightmares US*. I'm especially pleased about this: it'll show some of my American critics what I'm about, the passion for excellence that motivates me. I will feel vindicated, and I hope that Frank Bruni, over whom I've lost so much sleep, will watch. Meanwhile, we press on with *Hell's Kitchen US*. In the next series, contestants will have to cook dishes just like 'mother used to make'. The panel of judges will comprise their mothers, and my mum will be its chairwoman.

Finally, there is a possibility that *Humble Pie* will become, as they say, a major motion picture. I've been approached by some amazing guys who see it as a kind of Billy Elliot-style film, only with chef's whites rather than ballet shoes; the climax will be our young hero picking up his first Michelin star. It seems unimaginable, really, that this book, which was sometimes so painful to write, could ever be turned into something for the big screen, because I didn't set out to do anything other than set the record straight. But it seems that, somewhere along the way, people recognised aspects of themselves in my story. Perhaps they connected with my struggle; perhaps they just respected my determination. If that's so, I couldn't be more pleased. But for my own part, it's a relief just to be able to be myself.

PICTURE CREDITS

All photographs have been supplied by the author, with the exception of:

A.C Cooper: page 7 (top); Capital Pictures: page 21 (bottom); Danny Lawson/PA/Empics: page 24 (top); Denman Repros: page 3; Eddie Monsoon/Camera Press: page 17; EPA/Gerry Penny/ Corbis: page 14 (bottom); Getty Images: page 23 (top); Glen Dearing/Eyevine: page 19 (bottom) and page 22 (top and middle); John Paul Brooke: page 14 (top) and page 24 (bottom); John Sibley/Action Images: page 23 (bottom); Karwai Tang/Alpha Press: page 22 (bottom); Mirrorpix: page 13 (bottom) and page 21 (top); Monitor Photography Limited National: page 9 (top); Neil Wilder/IPG/Katz/Corbis: page 16; Peter Macdiarmid/Rex Features: page 18 (top); Rex Features: page 13 (top), page 15 (top, middle and bottom); Richard Young/Rex: page 18; Richard Young/ Rex Features: page 10 (bottom); The Estate of Bob Carlos Clarke: page 10 (top); Tim Rooke/Rex Features: page 19 (bottom)

While every effort has been made to trace the owners of copyright material reproduced herein, the publishers would like to apologise for any omissions and will be pleased to incorporate missing acknowledgements in any future correspondence.

INDEX